Handling Rowing Boats

A Collection of Historical Boating Articles on Launching, Oarsmanship, Steering and Other Aspects of Rowing

By

Various Authors

British Library Cataloguing-in-Publication Data
A catalogue record for this book is available from
the British Library

Contents

Rowing

ROWING is technically defined as the act of propelling a boat, by two or more persons, by means of a succession of strokes of oars. For our purpose, however, we will take the term also to include sculling by one person with sculls (or light oars).

As a sport, rowing has long been popular in this country. In fact, the first race was rowed by six Thames Watermen in 1715 for Doggett's Coat and Badge, awarded by Thomas Doggett, an actor, in honour of George I's accession. The prize consisted of a red coat with a large silver badge on the arm. The race was rowed on a course which extended from London Bridge to Chelsea, and still takes place annually under the auspices of the Fishmongers' Company.

From this beginning, rowing became a favourite sport, and university and school boat races, and river regattas were held. Then, gradually, the lightweight, perfectly balanced racing boats were evolved. They seated eight, six, four, two or one oarsmen, and with these improved craft, rowing gained even wider popularity. Today rowing is a major sport, and, in the spring and early summer, races and regattas are held on most rivers.

It is, of course, comparatively easy to row a boat after a fashion, but high-speed and long distance work have necessitated a skilful technique. To achieve success the most efficient strokes must be made, with the least effort; and every muscle, and ounce of strength, must be used to the best advantage.

You will find it easier to learn the correct stroke, if you make up a crew with some friends and each take one oar.

Wherever possible, practise your strokes while the boat is moored to a bank or jetty. Let the starboard oarsmen practise first, taking their time from their leader or stroke.

Each oarsman should settle himself comfortably on the seat, or thwart with his back to the bows. In front of him is the rowlock in which he will place his oar, and at his feet—fitted into grooves at the bottom of the boat is a wooden foot-rest, or stretcher.

Sea Cadets at Boat Practice

First see that your stretcher is in the right position. You will have a choice of three or four grooves into which it will fit, so place it where it will provide resistance to your feet as you swing back to make your stroke— that is when your legs will be almost fully stretched.

2

Next, ship your oars into position in the rowlock so that the shaped part, below the grip, fits against the support. Then, taking your time from your leader, swing forward, at the same time giving a slight twist to your wrist to bring the blade of the oar back into a position horizontal to the water. This is known as 'feathering.' It lessens the wind resistance to your oars by reducing the surface on which the wind can blow. This is a great advantage in a high wind, or when speed is important.

Let your blade enter the water almost vertically (inclined a fraction aft) with as little splash as possible, then pull the loom back strongly. Try to make a long, steady stroke when rowing on smooth water, and take the blade just far enough below the surface to get a good pull against the water. If you drive your oar too deep it will make your task heavier and will also slow the speed of your boat. On the other hand if your stroke is too shallow the water will not offer enough resistance and you may "catch a crab" and topple backwards, doing a nautical version of Knees-up Mother Brown!

When rowing in a choppy sea, you will find you make better progress if you use short, quick strokes, because this lessens the possibility of your oars becoming high and dry when you fall into a trough between waves.

After each oarsman has practised his stroke you can cast off and try your skill in the open water. If your boat has a rudder, the coxswain should take his seat by the rudder lines, ready to swing the boat away from the side. The coxswain is in charge of the boat and it is his responsibility to give correct orders to the oarsmen. His orders should always be given when the blades of the oars are still in the water. Then the oarsmen make one further stroke before carrying out the order. This enables them all to work together easily.

When the cox says *"Oars"* the crew should have their oars at the ready in the rowlocks with their blades parallel to the surface of the water.

The boat is then shoved off and the cox gives the order: *"Give way together."* This means that the crew, taking the time from the stroke oar, start to pull. *"Way enough"* is the order to stop pulling. *"Boat your oars"* is the command used to tell the crew to unship their oars from the rowlocks and lay them fore and aft in the boat.

3

The next command will probably be "*Oars ready*" which means that the oars should be replaced in the rowlocks. Then will follow "*Oars*" and "*Give way Together.*" If the cox wants to stop the progress of the boat he will say "*Hold water.*" The blades of the oars are then held firmly in the water, at right angles to the boat so that they act as a brake.

To turn the boat around quickly, the order will be "*Back Starboard*" or "*Back Port.*" Then the oarsmen on the side indicated will make their stroke backwards (that is, they will swing the blades of their oars forward, out of the water, bring them down and pull them back through the water in the opposite direction to that customary when they are giving way). The oarsmen on the opposite side continue to row in the usual manner. "*Back Starboard*" has the effect of turning the boat to starboard.

If it is necessary to move the boat astern, the cox should say "*Back Together*" when both port and starboard oarsmen will back their oars in the way described.

Those are the basic commands used when the boat is carrying a crew of four or more and cox. If you want to put up a really efficient show, you can go further and learn to "*Toss your oars,*" naval fashion. This order is given when coming alongside, and is put into effect by bringing the oars inboard and holding them in a vertical position, with the blades in the air, fore and aft.

If you are not lucky enough to find a crew with whom to practice, you can have a lot of fun learning to row with only one companion, taking an oar each and steering the boat by means of the oars.

In this case it will be the responsibility of the one nearest the bows to glance over his shoulder and keep a look-out for obstructions and changes of course. He will then give instructions to his companion using the fore-going commands for clarity. To steer a rudderless boat to starboard, row with your port oar. To steer to port, use your starboard oar. Remember that these instructions are concerned with port and starboard as the left and right of the boat facing the bows, whereas you will row facing the stern.

When you progress to rowing alone, your main difficulty will probably be the synchronisation of your strokes. To overcome this, keep your hands fairly close together as you swing forward and make sure that you pull back evenly with both arms.

There are several safety rules to be observed when rowing. The first of these has already been mentioned in the chapter on canoeing, but it applies equally to all craft and cannot be over-stressed. It is, briefly, that non-swimmers should never venture out of their depth in any boat. Another point to watch is that you always keep the weight of your passengers and crew evenly distributed in the boat, and do not allow any standing up in a narrow boat. An inexperienced passenger may stand up to change places or to get a better view of the scenery and cause the boat to wobble. Then he—or more probably she!—may panic, clutch at someone else and capsize the boat.

In the Royal Navy, there is a rule that the crew keep their hands inside the boat and clear of the gunwale. This is very important. Clutching at the gunwale as you go alongside a jetty or another boat may result in you crushing your fingers and being out of action for weeks.

Especially if the boat is your own, you will want to keep it as spick and span as possible and will try to avoid getting any scratches on its side. To avoid scratches when coming alongside, fit your boat with rope "fenders" which you can buy from a yacht outfitter. They normally hang inboard, and are swung over the side before landing. These fenders then come between the side of the boat and the jetty and act as buffers, preventing the side of the boat from scraping against the landing place.

Always remember when on a river, that rowing down-stream is comparatively easy. But when you row back against the current, and possibly against a high wind, you may find that every mile rowed up-stream equals in effort, two or more miles downstream. Moral: don't go cruising too far down the river on a windy afternoon!

If you are boating on the sea, try to find out all about the local currents or tide-races. It isn't clever to go nearer the danger area than the other fellow. What begins as a light-hearted dare, may end up with you being swept helplessly out to sea, or worse still—against the rocks. Make a particular point of watching the tides. Rowing out to sea on an ebb-tide is even more deceptive than rowing down-stream on a river. It's easy to go out, but perhaps impossible to get back—without the lifeboat!

Never put out to sea in a boat without a bailing-can and make sure that the oars are sound and the boat sea-worthy before you start. Experienced boatmen are always careful about these points; it is the amateur sailor who is the chief-offender, so if you borrow a boat from a friend who is a beginner, remember to check its soundness.

If you ever have the misfortune to lose an oar while rowing on the sea, put the remaining oar over the stern—where there may be a rowlock, or a hole for a metal crutch—and propel the boat by sculling. This calls for skill and "knack," and you will need some practice near the shore before you will be able to use this method efficiently.

Rowing is one of the most nautical accomplishments, because, even if you graduate to an ocean-going yacht, you are never free of the oars. In fact, the larger your yacht, the more dependent you are on your rowing-dinghy which you will use for coming ashore and for carrying provisions. Large yachts have to moor in deep water and so they use rowing-boats as tenders.

When mooring a small boat, either haul the boat above high-water mark, or secure her to a jetty, taking care to make her painter fast either to another boat or pontoon. On an ebb tide you must be sure that there is a long enough scope of line to prevent her being left hanging by the bows.

If the range of tide is considerable, the best way to moor a boat is to anchor her in deep water on a long enough scope of cable to allow her stern just to reach the jetty or beach; then carry a good sternfast well out along the beach or jetty.

Well, if you can remember and put into practice all that I have told you in this chapter, you are on the way to becoming a first-class seaman. Next I intend to take you a step further and to embark on the most difficult and fascinating of all boating pursuits—the adventure of sailing. So boat those oars—and up with the mainsail!

BISHAM COURT.

SCIENTIFIC OARSMANSHIP.

ʳ a thing is worth doing at all it is worth doing well, whether
be undertaken in sport or as a means of livelihood.

The first principles of oarsmanship may be explained to a
ᵉginner in a few minutes, and he might roughly put them
ₜo force, in a casual and faulty manner, on the first day of
ᵢs education.

In all pastimes and professions there is, as even a child
ₙows, a very wide difference between the knowing how a thing
done and the rendering of the operation in the most approved
ₙd scientific manner.

In all operations which entail the use of implements there
ʳe three essentials to the attainment of real merit in the opera-
ₒn. These are, firstly, physical capacitý ; secondly, good tools

7

to work with ; thirdly, practice and painstaking on the part of the student.

For the purposes of the current chapter we shall postulate the two former, and confine the theme to details of such study and practice of oarsmanship as are requisite in order to attain scientific use of oars or sculls.

When commencing to learn an operation which entails a new and unwonted exercise, distinct volition is necessary on the part of the brain, in order to dictate to the various muscles the parts which they are to play in the operation.

The oftener that a muscular movement is repeated the less intense becomes the mental volition which is required to dictate that movement ; until at last the movement becomes almost mechanical, and can be reproduced without a strain of the will (so long as the muscular power is not exhausted).

One object of studied practice at any given muscular movement is to accustom the muscles to this particular function, until they become capable of carrying it out without requiring specific and laborious instructions from the headquarters of the brain on the occasion of each such motion. Another object and result of exercise of one or more sets of muscles is to develop their powers. The anatomical reasons why muscles increase in vigour and activity under exercise need not be here discussed ; the fact may be accepted that they do so.

Hence, by practice of any kind of muscular movement, the student increases both the vigour and the independence of action of the muscles concerned.

In any operation with implements there is some one method of performing the same which experience has proved to be the most effectual for the purpose required. There will be other methods, or variations of method, which will attain a somewhat similar but less effectual and less satisfactory result.

It requires distinct volition in the first instance to perform the operation in an inferior manner, just as it does to perform it in the most approved manner, to perform ' clumsily ' or to perform ' cleverly.'

Naturally, if the volition to act clumsily be repeated a sufficient number of times, the muscles learn independent clumsy action with as much facility as they would have otherwise acquired independent clever and scientific action. Hence the importance of knowing which is the most approved and effectual method of setting to work, and of being informed of the result, good or bad, of each attempt, while the volition is still in active force, and before the 'habit' of muscular action, perfect or imperfect, is fully formed.

We all know that, whether we are dealing with morals or with muscles, it is a matter of much difficulty to overcome a bad habit, and to form a different and a better one relating to the same course of action.

When the pupil begins to learn to row the brain has many things to think of ; it has several orders to distribute simultaneously to its different employés—the various muscles required for the work—and these employés are, moreover, 'new to the business.' They have not yet, from want of practice, developed the vigour and strength which they will require hereafter ; and also they know so little of what they have to do that they require incessant instruction from brain headquarters, or else they make blunders. But in time both master and servants, brain and muscles, begin to settle down to their business. The master becomes less confused, and gives his orders with more accuracy and less oblivion of details ; the servants acquire more vigour, and pick up the instructions with more facility. At last the time comes when the servants know pretty well what their master would have them do, and act spontaneously, while the master barely whispers his orders, and has leisure to attend to other matters, or at all events saves himself the exertion of having momentarily to shout his orders through a speaking-trumpet. Meantime, as said before, the servants can only obey orders ; and, if their original instructions have been blunders on the part of the master, they settle down to the reproduction of these blunders.

Now it often happens that an oarsman, who is himself a

good judge of rowing, and is capable of giving very good instructions to others, is guilty of many faults in his own oarsmanship. And yet it cannot be said of him that he 'knows no better' as regards those faults which he personally commits. On the contrary, if he were to see one of his own pupils rowing with any one of these same faults, he would promptly detect it, and would be able to explain to the pupil the why and the wherefore of the error, and of its cure. Nevertheless, he perpetrates in his own person the very fault which he discerns and corrects when he notes it in another! And the reason is this. His own oarsmanship has become mechanical, and is reproduced stroke after stroke without a distinct volition. It became faulty at the time when it was becoming mechanical, because the brain was not sufficiently conscious of the orders which it was dictating, or was not duly informed, from some external source, what orders it should issue. So the brain gave wrong orders, through carelessness or ignorance, or both, and continued to repeat them, until the muscles learnt to repeat their faulty functions spontaneously, and without the immediate cognisance of the brain.

This illustration, of which many a practical instance will be recalled by any rowing man of experience, serves to show the importance of keeping the mind attentive, as far as possible, at all times when rowing, and still more so while elementary rowing is being learnt, and also of having, if possible, a mentor to watch the endeavours of the student, and to inform him of any error of movement which he may perpetrate, before his mind and muscles become confirmed in an erroneous line of action.

The reader will therefore see from the above that it is important for any one who seeks to acquire really scientific oarsmanship, not only to pay all the mental attention that he can to the movements which he is executing, but also to secure the presence of some experienced adviser who will watch the execution of each stroke, and will point out at the time what movements have been correctly and what have been incorrectly performed.

Having shown the importance of careful study and tuition in the details of scientific oarsmanship, we now enter into those details themselves, but still confine ourselves to what is known as 'fixed' seat rowing, taking them separately, and dealing first with the stroke itself, as distinct from the 'recovery' between the strokes.

While carrying out the stroke upon general principles, the oarsman, in order to produce a maximum effect with a relatively minimum expenditure of strength, has to study the following details :

1. To keep the back rigid, and to swing from the hips.

2. To maintain his shoulders braced when the oar grasps the water.

3. To use the legs and feet in the best manner and at the exact instant required.

4. To hold his oar properly.

5. To govern the depth of the blade with accuracy, including the first dip of the blade into the water to the moment when the blade quits it.

6. To row the stroke home to his chest, bending his arms neither too soon nor too late.

7. To do so with the correct muscles.

8. To drop the hands and elevate the oar from the water in the right manner and at the right moment.

Then again, when the stroke is completed and the recovery commences, the details to be further observed are :

9. To avoid 'hang' or delay of action either with hands or body.

10. To manipulate the feather with accuracy and at the proper instant.

11. To govern the height of the blade during the recovery.

12. To use the legs and feet correctly and at the right moments of recovery.

13. To keep the button of the oar home to the thowl.

14. To regulate the proportionate speeds of recovery of arms and of body, relatively to each other.

15. To return the feathered oar to the square position at the right time and in the correct manner.

16. To raise the hands at the right moment, and so to lower the blade into the water at the correct instant.

17. To recommence the action of the new stroke at the right instant.

These several details present an apparently formidable list of detailed studies to be followed in order to execute a series of strokes and recoveries in the most approved fashion. In performance the operation is far more homogeneous than would appear from the above disjointed analysis of the several movements to be performed. The division of movements is made for the purpose of observation and appreciation of possibly several faults, which may occur in any one of the movements detailed. As a fact, the correct rendering of one movement— of one detail of the stroke—facilitates correctness in succeeding or contemporaneous details ; while, on the other hand, a faulty rendering of one movement tends to hamper the action of the body in other details, and to make it more liable to do its work incorrectly in some or all of them. Experience shows that one fault, in one distinct detail, is constantly the primary cause of a concatenation of other faults. To set the machine in incorrect motion in one branch of it tends to put the whole, or the greater part of it, more or less out of gear, and to cripple its action from beginning to end of the chapter.

Taking these various details *seriatim*.

1. The back should be set stiff, and preserved stiff throughout the stroke. Obviously, if the back yields to the strain, the stroke is not so effectual. Besides, if the back is badly humped the expansion of the chest is impeded ; and with this the action of the pectoral muscles and of the shoulders (of both of which more anon) is also fettered. Further, the lungs have less freedom of play when the back is bent and the chest cramped ; and the value of free respiration requires no explanation.

We have said that the back must be stiff. If the back can be straight, from first to last, stiffness is ensured, *ipso facto*. If the back is bent, care must be taken that the bend does not increase or decrease during the stroke ; whether straight or bent, the back should be rigid.

The conformation and development of the muscles of the back are not quite the same in all subjects. With some persons absolute straightness of back comes almost naturally ; with others the attainment of straightness is not a matter of much difficulty. With others, again, a slight amount of curve in the back is more natural under the strain of the oar, even with all attention and endeavour to keep the back flat. With such as these any artificial straightening of the back, that places it in a position in which the muscles, as they are adapted to the frame, have not the fullest and freest play, detracts from rather than adds to the power of the oarsman.

But in all cases it is important that the back, whether straight or slightly arched, should be rigid, and should swing from the hips. If the swing takes place from one or more of the vertebræ of the spine, the force which the oarsman can by such actions produce is far less than would be the case if he kept his spine rigid and had swung to and fro from his hips.

In order to facilitate the entire body in swinging from the hips, and not from one of the vertebræ, the legs should be opened, and the knees induced outward, as the body swings forward. The body can then lower itself to a greater reach forward, and directly from the hips ; whereas if the knees are placed together the thighs check the forward motion of the body, and compel it, if it remains rigid, to curtail its forward reach. (If the vertebræ bend when the swing from the hips is checked by the bent knees, the extra reach thus attained is weak, and of comparatively minor effect.)

Next (2) the shoulders have to be rigid. If they give way, and if the sockets stretch when the strain of the oar is felt, the effect of the stroke is evidently weakened. Now if the shoulders are stretched forward at the beginning of the stroke, the muscles which govern and support them have not the same power of rigidity that they possess when the shoulders are well drawn back at the outset. The oarsman gains a little in reach by extending his shoulders, but he loses in rigidity of muscle, and consequently in the force which he applies to the oar.

3. The legs and feet should combine to exercise pressure against the stretcher at the same moment, and contemporaneously with the application of the oar to the water. If they press too soon, the body is forced back while the oar is in air; if too late, the hold of the water is weak, for want of legwork to support the body.

4. The oar should be held in the fingers, not in the fist; the lower joints of the fingers should be nearly straight when the oar is held. The hold which a gymnast would take of a bar of the same thickness, if he were hanging from it, is, as regards the four fingers of the hand, the same which an oarsman should take of his oar. His thumb should come underneath, not over the handle.

5 and 10. Government of the depression or elevation of the blade, respectively, during stroke and recovery, is a matter of application of joints and of muscles. This much may be borne in mind, that the freer the wrist is, the better is the oar governed; and if an oar is clutched in the fist the flexibility of the wrist is thereby much crippled.

6. The arms should begin to bend when the body has just found the perpendicular. The upper arm should swing close to the ribs, worked by the shoulders, which should be thrown well back.

7. The 'biceps' should not do the work; for, if it does, either the hands are elevated or the level of the blade altered—if the elbows keep close to the side; or else, if the level of the hands is preserved, then the elbows dog's-ear outwards. In either case the action is less free and less powerful than if the stroke is rowed home by the shoulder muscles.

8. The part of the hand which should touch the chest when the oar comes home is the root of the thumb, not the knuckles of the fingers. If the knuckles touch the chest *before* the oar

comes out of water, the blade is 'feathered under water'—a common fault, and a very insidious one. If, on the other hand, the oar comes out clean, but the first thing which touches the chest is the knuckle, then the last part of the stroke will have been rowed in *air*, and not in *the water*.

9. Dealing now with recovery. The hands should rebound from the chest like a billiard-ball from a cushion. If the hands delay at the chest they hamper the recovery of the body—e.g. let any man try to push a weight away from him with his hands and body combined. He will find that, if he pushes with straight arms, he is better able to apply the weight of his body to the forward push than if he keeps his arms bent.

Having shot his hands away, and having straightened his arms as quickly as he reasonably can, his body should follow ; but his body should not meantime have been stationary. It should, like a pendulum, begin to swing for the return so soon as the stroke is over.

If hands 'hang,' the body tends to hang, as above shown ; and if the body hangs, valuable time is lost, which can never be regained. As an illustration : suppose a man is rowing forty strokes in a minute, and that his body hangs the tenth of a second when it is back after each stroke, then at the end of a minute's rowing he will have sat still for four whole seconds ! An oarsman who has no hang in his recovery can thus row a fast stroke with less exertion to himself than one who hangs. The latter, having wasted time between stroke and recovery, has to swing forward all the faster, when once he begins to recover, in order to perform the same number of strokes in the same time as he who does not hang. Now, although there is a greater effort required to row the blade square through the water than to recover it edgewise through the air, yet the latter has to be performed with muscles so much weaker for the task set to them that relatively they tire sooner under their lighter work than do the muscles which are in use for rowing the blade through the water. When an oarsman becomes 'pumped,' he feels the task of recovery even more severe than that of

rowing the stroke. Hence we see the importance of econo-
mising as far as possible the labour of those muscles which are
employed on the recovery, and of not adding to their toil by
waste of time which entails a subsequent extra exertion in
order to regain lost ground and lost time.

10. The manipulation of the blade through the water is
of great importance, otherwise the blade will not keep square,
and regular pressure against the water will not be attained.
Now, since the angle of the blade to the water has to be a
constant one, and since the plane on which the blade works
also is required to be uniform, till the moment for the feather
has arrived, it stands to reason that the wrists and arms, which
are changing their position relatively with the body while the
stroke progresses, must accommodate themselves to the pro-
gressive variations of force of body and arms, so as to maintain
the uniform angle and plane of the oar. Herein much attention must be paid to maxim 4 (*supra*). If an oar is held in the
fist instead of in the fingers, the play of the muscles of the
wrist is thereby crippled, and it becomes less easy to govern
the blade.

11. On a somewhat similar principle as the foregoing, the
arms, on the recovery, are changing their position and angle
with the body throughout the recovery ; but the blade has to
be kept at a normal level above the water all the time. It is
a common fault for the oarsman to fail to regulate the height
of the feather, and either to ' toss ' it at some point of the recovery
or else to lower it till the blade almost, if not quite, touches
the water. Nothing but practice, coupled with careful obser-
vations of the correct manner of holding an oar, can attain that
mechanical give-and-take play of muscles which produces an
even and clean feather from first to last of recovery.

12. We are still, for the sake of argument, dealing with
fixed-seat oarsmanship. Slides will be discussed subsequently.

In using the legs, on a fixed seat, for recovery, the toes
should feel the strap, which should cross them on or below the
knuckle-joint of the great toe. Each foot should feel and pull

up the strap easily and simultaneously, so as to preserve even position of body. The legs should open well, and allow the body to trick between them as it swings forward.

13. If the body swings true, the oar will keep home to the rowlock ; there should be just sufficient fraction of weight pressed against the button to keep it home ; if it is suffered to leave the rowlock, the oarsman tends to screw outwards over the gunwale, and also, when he recommences the stroke, he loses power by reason of his oar not meeting with its due support until the abstracted button has slipped back against the thowl.

14. The pace of recovery should be proportionate to the speed of stroke. If recovery is too slow, the oarsman becomes late in getting into the water for the next stroke ; if he is too quick, he has to wait when forward in order not to hurry the stroke.

15. Too many even high-class oars are prone to omit to keep the oar feathered for the full distance of the recovery. They have a tendency to turn it square too soon. By so doing they incur extra resistance of air and extra labour on the recovery, and they are more liable to foul a wave in rough water. The oar should be carried forwards edgewise, and only turned square just as full reach is attained. It should then be turned sharply, and not gradually.

16. The instant the body is full forward, and the oar set square, the hands should be raised sharply to the exact amount required in order to drop the blade into the water to the required depth, so as to cover it for the succeeding stroke.

17. The new stroke should be recommenced without delay, by throwing the body sharply back, with arms stiff and shoulders braced, the legs pressing firmly and evenly against the stretcher, so as to take the weight of the body off the seat, and to transfer its support to the handle of the oar and the stretcher, thus making the very most of weight and of extensor muscles in order to give force to the oar against the water.

N.B. Before closing these remarks, it should be added that,

with reference to detail 12, it is assumed that the oarsman, having progressed to the scientific stage, has so far mastered the use of the loins as to be able to combine their action with that of the toe against the strap in aiding the recovery of the body. If he tries to rely solely on the motor power for recovery from the strap, and the toes against it, he will not swing forward with a stiff back, and will be in a slouched position when he attains his reach forward.

The Rev. E. Warre, D.D., published in 1875 some brief remarks upon the stroke, in a treatise upon physical exercises and recreations. They are here reproduced by leave, the writer feeling that they can hardly be surpassed for brevity and lucidity of instruction upon the details of the stroke.

NOTES ON THE STROKE.

The moment the oar touches the body, drop the hands smartly straight down, then turn the wrists sharply and at once shoot out the hands in a straight line to the front, inclining the body forward from the thigh-joints, and simultaneously bring up the slider, regulating the time by the swing forward of the body according to the stroke. Let the chest and stomach come well forward, the shoulders be kept back ; the inside arm be straightened, the inside wrist a little raised, the oar grasped in the hands, but not pressed upon more than is necessary to maintain the blade in its proper straight line as it goes back ; the head kept up, the eyes fixed on the outside shoulder of the man before you. As the body and arms come forward to their full extent, the wrists having been quickly turned, the hands must be raised sharply, and the blade of the oar brought to its full depth at once. At that moment, without the loss of a thousandth part of a second, the whole weight of the body must be thrown on to the oar and the stretcher, by the body springing back, so that the oar may catch hold of the water sharply, and be driven through it by a force unwavering and uniform. As soon as the oar has got hold of the water, and the beginning of the stroke has been effected as described, flatten the knees, and so, using the muscles of the legs, keep up the pressure of the beginning uniform through the backward motion of the body. Let the arms be rigid at the beginning of the stroke. When the body reaches the perpendicular, let the elbows be bent and dropped close past the sides to the rear

—the shoulders dropping and disclosing the chest to the front ; the back, if anything, curved inwards rather than outwards, but not strained in any way. The body, in fact, should assume a natural upright sitting posture, with the shoulders well thrown back. In this position the oar should come to it and the feather commence.

N.B.—It is important to remember that the body should never stop still. In its motion backwards and forwards it should imitate the pendulum of a clock. When it has ceased to go forward it has begun to go back.

There are, it will appear, from consideration of the directions, about twenty-seven distinct points, *articuli* as it were, of the stroke. No one should attempt to coach a crew without striving to obtain a practical insight into their nature and order of succession. Let a coxswain also remember that, in teaching men to row, his object should be to teach them to economise their *strength* by using properly their *weight*. Their weight is always in the boat along with them ; their strength, if misapplied, very soon evaporates

MARLOW.

COACHING.

FOR reasons which were set forth at the commencement of the chapter on scientific oarsmanship, the very best oar may fail to see his own faults. For this reason, in dealing with the methods for detecting and curing faults, it seems more to the point to write as addressing the tutor rather than the pupil. The latter will improve faster under any adequate verbal instruction than by perusing pages of bookwork upon the science of oarsmanship.

A coach may often know much more than he can himself perform ; he may be with his own muscles but a mediocre exponent of his art, and yet be towards the top of the tree as regards know-ledge and power of instruction.

A coach, like his pupils, often becomes too ‘ mechanical ’ ; he sees some salient fault in his crew, he sets himself to eradicate it, and meanwhile it is possible that he may overlook some other great fault which is gradually developing itself among one or more of the men. And yet if he were asked to coach some other crew for the day, in which crew this same fault existed, he would be almost certain to note it, and to set to work to cure it.

For this reason, although it does not do to have too many mentors at work from day to day upon one crew, nevertheless the best of coaches may often gain a hint by taking some one else into his counsels for an hour or two, and by comparing notes.

We have said that it is not absolutely necessary that a good coach should always be in his own person a finished oarsman ; but if he is all the better, and for one very important reason. More than half the faults which oarsmen contract are to be traced in the first instance to some irregularity in the machinery with which they are working. That irregularity may be of two sorts, direct or indirect—direct when the boat, oar, rowlock, or stretcher is improperly constructed, so that an oarsman cannot work fairly and squarely ; indirect when some other oarsman is perpetrating some fault which puts others out of gear.

If a coach is a good oarsman on his own account (by 'good' we mean scientific rather than merely powerful), he can and should test and try or inspect the seat and oar of each man whom he coaches, especially if he finds a man painstaking and yet unable to cure some special fault. Boatbuilders are very careless in laying out work. A rowlock may be too high or too low ; it may rake one way or other, and so spoil the plane of the oar in the water. An oar may be hog-backed (or sprung), or too long in loom, or too short ; the straps of a stretcher may be fixed too high, so as to grip only the tip of a great-toe, and the place for the feet may not be straight to the seat, or a rowlock may be too narrow, and so may jam the oar when forward.

These are samples of mechanical discomfort which may spoil

any man's rowing, and against which it may be difficult for the most painstaking pupil to contend successfully. If the coach is good in practice as well as in theory of oarsmanship, he can materially simplify his own labours and those of his pupils by inspecting and trying the 'work' of each man in turn.

He should bear in mind that if a young oar is thrown out of shape in his early career by bad mechanical appliances, the faults of shape often cling to him unconsciously later on, even when he is at last furnished with proper tools. If a child were taught to walk with one boot an inch thicker in the sole than the other, the uneven gait thereby produced might cling to him long after he had been properly shod.

Young oarsmen in a club are too often relegated to practise in cast-off boats with cast-off oars, none of which are really fit for use. Nothing does more to spoil the standard of junior oarsmanship in a club than neglect of this nature.

Having ascertained that all his pupils are properly equipped and are properly seated, fair and square to stretchers suitable for the length of leg of each, the next care of a coach should be to endeavour to trace the *cause* of each fault which he may detect. This is more difficult than to see that a fault exists. At the same time, if the coach cannot trace the cause, it is hardly reasonable to expect the pupil to do so. So many varied causes may produce some one generic fault that it may drive a pupil from one error to another to tell him nothing more than that he is doing something wrong without at the same time explaining to him how and why he is at fault.

For instance, suppose a man gets late into the water. This lateness may arise from a variety of causes, for example :

1. He may be hanging with arms or body, or both, when he has finished the stroke, and so he may be late in starting to go forward ; or

2. He may be correct until he has attained his forward reach, and then, may be, he hangs before dropping his oar into the water ; or

3. He may begin to drop his oar at the right time, but to do

so in a 'clipping' manner, not dropping the oar perpendicularly, but bringing it for some distance back in the air before it touches the water.

Now to tell a batch of men—all late, and all late from different causes as above—simply that each one is 'late' does little good. The cure which will set the one right will only vary, or even exaggerate, the mischief with the others.

Hence a coach should, before he animadverts upon a fault, of which he observes the effect, watch carefully until he detects the exact cause, and then seek to eradicate it.

Another sample of cause and effect in faults may be cited for illustration. Suppose a man holds his oar in his fist instead of his fingers. The effect of this probably will be a want of accuracy in 'governing' the blade. He may thereby row too deep ; also only half feather ; also find a difficulty in bending his wrists laterally, and therefore fail to bring his elbows neatly past his sides. The consequent further effect may well be that he dog's-ears his elbows and gets a cramped finish. This will tend to make his hands come slow off the chest for the recovery ; and this again may tend to make his body heavy on the return swing.

Here is a pretty, and quite possible, concatenation of faults all bearing on each other in sequence, more or less. To be scolded for each such fault in turn may well bewilder a pupil. He will be taken aback at the plurality of defects which he is told to cure. But if the coach should spot the faulty grip, and cure that by some careful coaching in a tub-gig, he may in a few days find the other faults gradually melt away when the one primary awkwardness has been eradicated.

These two illustrations of faults and their origins by no means exhaust the category of errors which a coach has to detect and to cure.

Sundry other common faults may be specified, and the best mode of dealing with them by coaches supplied.

Over-reach of shoulders.—This weakens the catch of the water, and also tends to cripple the finish when the time comes to row the oar home. The shoulders should be braced well back. The extra inch or less of forward reach which the over-reach obtains is not worth having at the cost of weakening the catch and cramping the finish. The fault is best cured by gig-coaching and by demonstrating in person the correct and the wrong poses of the shoulders.

Meeting the oar.—This may come from more than one cause. If the legs leave off supporting the body before the oar-handle comes to the chest, the body droops to the strain from want of due support ; or if the oarsman tries to row the stroke home with arms only, ceasing the swing back ; and still more, if he tries to finish with biceps instead of by shoulder muscles, he is not unlikely to row deep, because he feels the strain of rowing the oar home in time, with less power behind it than that employed by others in the boat. He finds the oar come home easier if it is slightly deflected, and so unconsciously he begins to row rather deep (or light) at the finish, in order to get his oar home at the right instant.

Swing—faults of may be various. There may be a hang, or conversely a hurry, in the swing ; and, as shown above, the causes of these errors in swing may often be beneath the surface, and be connected with faulty hold of an oar, or a loose or badly placed strap, or a stretcher of wrong length, or from faulty finish of the preceding stroke. Lateness in swing may arise *per se*, and so may a ' bucket,' but as often as not they are linked with other faults, which have to be corrected at least simultaneously, and often antecedently.

Screwing either arises from mechanical fault at the moment or from former habits of rowing under difficulties occasionally with bad appliances. If a man sits square, with correct oar, rowlock, and stretcher, he does not naturally screw. If the habit seems to have grown upon him, a change of side will often do more than anything else to cure him. He is screwing because he is working his limbs and loins unevenly ; hence the obvious policy of making him change the side on which he puts the greater pressure.

Feather under water.—The fault is one of the most common, the remedy simple. The pupil should be shown the difference between turning the oar-handle before he drops it (as he is doing) and of dropping it before he turns it as he ought to do ; and it should be impressed upon him that the root of the thumb, and not his knuckles, should touch his chest when the oar comes home, and should be done *before*, and not after, he has dropped his handle to elevate the blade from the water.

If a crew feather much under water, it is a good plan to seat them in a row on a bench, and give each man a stick to handle as an oar. Then make them very slowly follow the actions of the coach, or a fugleman. 1. Hands up to the chest, root of thumb touching chest. 2. Drop the hands. 3. Turn them (as for feather) sharply. 4. Shoot them out, &c.

Having got them to perform each motion slowly and distinctly, then gradually accelerate the actions, until they are done as an entirety, with rapidity and *in proper consecution*. The desideratum is to ensure motion, No. 3 being performed in its due order, and *not before* No. 2.

Five minutes' drill of this sort daily before the rowing, for a week or two, will do much to cure feather under water even with hardened sinners.

Swing across the boat.—This is an insidious fault. The oarsman sits square, while his oar-handle moves in an arc of a circle. He has an instinctive tendency to endeavour to keep his chest square to his oar during the revolution of the latter. A No. 7 who has to take time from the stroke by the side of him is more prone than others to fall into this fault. The answer is, let the arms follow the action of the oar, and give way to it, and endeavour to keep the body straight and square. Keep the head well away from the oar, and its bias will tend to balance the swing.

Bending the arms prematurely is a common fault. Sometimes even high-class oars fall into it after a time. Tiros are prone to it, because they at first instinctively endeavour to work with arms rather than with body. Older oars adopt the trick in the endeavour to catch the water sharply at the beginning. Of course they lose power by doing so ; but they do not realise their loss, because, feeling a greater strain on their arms, they imagine that they must therefore be doing more work.

Lessons in a tub-gig are the best remedies for this fault.

'Paddling' is an art which is of much importance in order to bring a crew to perfection, and at the same time it is too often done in a slovenly manner compared with hard rowing.

The writer admits that his own views as to how paddling should be performed differ somewhat from those of sundry good judges and successful coaches. Some of these are of opinion that paddling should consist of rowing gently, comparatively speaking, with less force and catch at the beginning of the stroke and with less reach than when rowing hard, but with blade always covered to regulation depth. When the order is given to 'Row,' then the full length should be attained and the full 'catch' administered.

The writer's own version of paddling differs as follows. He is of opinion that the difference between paddling and rowing should be produced by working with a 'light'—only partially covered—blade when paddling. The effect of this is to ease the whole work of the stroke ; but at the same time the swing, reach, and catch should be just the same as if the blade were covered. Then, when the order comes to 'Row,' all the oarsman has to do is so to govern his blade that he now immerses the whole of it, and at the same time to increase his force to the amount necessary to row the stroke of the full blade throughout the required time.

Those good judges who differ from him as aforesaid base their objections to his method chiefly on the ground that it requires rather a higher standard of watermanship to enable an oarsman so to govern his blade that he can immerse it more or less at will, and yet maintain the same outward action of body, only with more or less force employed, according to amount of blade immersed.

The writer admits that his process does entail the acquisition of a somewhat higher standard of watermanship than the other system. But he is none the less of opinion that this admission should not be accepted as a ground for teaching the other style.

In the first place, it would seem to him better to try to raise the standard of watermanship to the system than to lower the system to meet the requirements of inferior skill. In the second, there seems to be even greater drawbacks to the system preferred by his friends who differ from him. For instance, under the alternative system the oarsman is taught to *alter* his style of body when paddling, but to maintain a uniform depth of blade. He is taught to apply less sharpness of catch, and less reach forward. To do so may tend to take the edge off catch, and to shorten reach, when hard rowing has to be recommenced.

It is plain that paddling cannot be all round the same as rowing ; there must be an alternative prescribed. The writer says, in effect : ‘ Alter only the blade (and so the amount of force required), and maintain outward action of body as before.’

Those who take the other view say, in effect : ‘ Maintain the same blade, and alter the action of the body.’

It must be admitted that those who differ from the writer are entitled, from their own performances as oarsmen and coaches, to every possible respect ; and the writer, while failing to agree with them, hesitates to assert that for that reason he must be right and they wrong.

One further reason in favour of paddling with a light blade may be added. When an oarsman is exhausted in a race, it is of supreme importance that, though unable to do his full share of work, he should not mar the swing and style of the rest. Now if such an oarsman, when nature fails him, can row lighter and so ease his toil, he can maintain swing and style with the rest. But if, on the other hand, he keeps his blade covered to the full, and seeks relief by rowing shorter and with less dash, he alters his style and tends to spoil the uniformity of the crew.

Watermanship is a quality which can hardly be coached ;

it may, therefore, seem out of place to deal with it under the head of coaching. Yet in one sense it pertains to coaching, because a mentor takes into calculation the capacity of an oarsman for exercising watermanship when making a selection of a crew.

Watermanship, as a technical term, may be said to consist in adapting oneself to circumstances and exigencies during the progress of a boat. A good waterman keeps time with facility, a bad one only after much painstaking—if at all. A good waterman adapts himself to every roll of the boat, sits tight to his seat, anticipates an incipient roll, and rights the craft so far as he can by altering his centre of gravity while yet plying his oar. A bad waterman is more or less helpless when a boat is off its keel, or when he encounters rough water. So long as the boat is level, he may be able to do even more work than the good waterman, but when the boat rolls he cannot help himself, still less can he right the ship and so help others to work, as can the good waterman.

Good watermen can jump into a racing boat and sit her offhand ; bad watermen will be unsteady in a keelless boat even after days of practice.

One or two good watermen are the making of a crew, especially when time is short for practice. They will raise the standard of rowing of all their colleagues, simply by keeping the balance of the boat. Sculling and pair-oar practice tend to teach watermanship. They induce a man to make use of his own back and beam in order to keep the boat on an even keel. We do not for this reason say that every tiro should be put to take lessons of watermanship in sculling-boats and light pairs : far from it. He will be likely in such craft to contract feather under water, and possibly screwing, in the efforts to obtain work on an even keel, after his own uneven action has conduced to rolling.

University men produce far fewer good watermen than the tideway clubs, and with good reason. The career on the river at Oxford or Cambridge is brief, and many a man goes out of residence while he is only on the threshold of aquatic science, both in practice and theory ; although, on account of his big frame, he may have been taught artificially to ply an oar, and with good effect, in a practised eight. Watermanship, like skating, cannot be acquired in a day, and the younger a man takes to aquatics the more likely is he to acquire it. There is hardly a bad waterman to be seen as a rule in a grand challenge crew of London R.C. or Thames R.C. men. Among University oars, watermanship is oftenest found in those who have rowed as schoolboys.

To coaches generally of the present and of future generations we may say that there is nothing like having a tenacity of purpose, and declining to listen to the shoals of excuses which pupils are inclined to propound in order to explain their shortcomings.

A SCRATCH EIGHT ('PEAL OF BELLS').

There should be no such thing as ' I can't' from a pupil. On the other hand, the coach should do his best to render the excuse untenable by ensuring proper 'work' at each thwart. A coach should not be carried away by every whisper of criticism by outsiders ; and yet at the same time he should realise as said at the beginning of this chapter, that, however able he may be, he has a natural tendency to become blind to faults which are being daily perpetrated under his nose—the more so if he has been specially of late devoting his attention to some different class of fault in his men. For this reason he should not decline to listen to suggestions from mentors who otherwise may be his inferiors in the art, and to give them all attention before he decides how to deal with them.

In dealing with the selection of men for a crew he has to consider various points. He has to calculate for what seats such and such an oarsman will be available, as regards weight and capacity generally for the seat. He has to bear in mind the date of the race for which he is preparing his men ; many an oarsman may be admittedly unfit for a seat if the race were rowed to-morrow, and yet he may show promise of being fit for it six months hence. A may be better than B to-day ; but A may be an old stager hardened in certain faults, and of whom no hope can now be entertained that he will suddenly reform. B may be as green as a gooseberry, and yet the recollection of what he was two or three weeks ago, compared to what he is now, may warrant the assumption that by the day of the race, some time hence, B will have become the better man of the two.

A coach who takes a crew in hand halfway through their preparation should be prepared to hear evidence as to what was the standard of merit of certain men some time back, compared with their present form ; otherwise he may delude himself as to the relative merits and prospects of the material which he has to mould into shape.

Just as orators are said to learn at the expense of their audience, so coaches do undoubtedly learn much at the expense of the crews which they manage. Many a coach will agree that he has often felt in later years that, if he had his time over again with this or that oarsman or crew, he would now form a different judgment from what he formerly did.

In concluding this chapter we cannot do better than extract from Dr. Warre's treatise on Athletics certain aphorisms for the benefit of coaches, which he has tersely compiled under the head of 'Notes on Coaching' :

NOTES ON COACHING.

In teaching a crew you have to deal with—

        A. Crew collectively.
        B. Crew individually.

A. *Collective.*

1. *Time.* —*a.* Oars in and out together. *b.* Feather, same height ; keep it down. *c.* Stroke, same depth ; cover the blades, but not above the blue.

2. *Swing.*—*a.* Bodies forward and back together. *b.* Sliders together. *c.* Eyes in the boat.

3. *Work.*—*a.* Beginning—together, sharp, hard. *b.* Turns of the wrist—on and off of the feather, sharp, but not too soon. *c.* Rise of the hands—sharp, just before stroke begins. *d.* Drop of the hands—sharp, just after it ends.

General Exhortations.—' Time !' ' Beginning !' 'Smite !' 'Keep it long !' and the like—to be given at the right moment, not used as mere parrot cries.

B. *Individual.*

1. Faults of position.

2 Faults of movement.

N.B.—These concern body, hands, arms, legs, and sometimes head and neck.

1. Point out when you easy, or when you come in, or best of all, in a gig. Show as well as say what is wrong and what is right.

N.B.—Mind you are right. *Decipit exemplar vitiis imitabile.*

2. To be pointed out during the row and corrected. Apply the principles taught in ' E. W.'s ' paper on the stroke, beginning with bow and working to stroke, interposing exhortations (A) at the proper time.

N.B.—Never hammer at any one individual. If one or two

admonitions don't bring him right, wait a bit and then try again. For coaching purposes, not too fast a stroke and not too slow. About thirty per minute is right. Before you start, see that your men have got their stretchers right and are sitting straight to their work.

He teaches best who, while he is teaching, remembers that he has much to learn.

BISHAM COURT REACH.

THE COXSWAIN AND STEERING.

THE 'cock-swain' wins his place chiefly on account of his weight, provided that he can show a reasonable amount of nerve and skill of hand. A coxswain is seldom a very practical oarsman, although there have been special exceptions to this rule, e.g. in the case of T. H. Marshall, of Exeter, Arthur Shadwell, of Oriel, and a few others. But if he has been any length of time at his trade he very soon picks up a very considerable theoretical knowledge of what rowing should be, and is able to do very signal service in the matter of instructing the men whom he pilots. When a youth begins to handle the rudder-lines there is often some considerable difficulty in inducing him to open his mouth to give orders of any sort. Even such biddings as to tell one side of oars to hold her, or another to row or to back-water, come at first falteringly from his lips. It is but natural that he should feel his own physical inferiority to the men whom he is for the moment required to order about so peremptorily, and diffidence at first tends to make him dumb. But he soon picks up his *rôle* when he listens to the audacious orders and objurgations of rival pilots, and he is pleased to find that the qualities of what he might modestly consider to be impudence and arrogance are the very things which are most required of him, and for the display of which he earns commendation.

Having once found his tongue, he soon learns to use it. When there is a coach in attendance upon the crew, the pilot is not called upon to animadvert on any failings of oarsmen ; but when the coach is absent the coxswain is bound to say something, and, if he has his wits about him, he soon picks up enough to make his remarks more or less to the purpose. The easiest detail on which he offers an opinion is that of time of oars. At first he feels guilty of ' cheek ' in singing out to some oarsmen of good standing that he is out of time. He feels as if he should hardly be surprised at a retort not to attempt to teach his grandmother ; but, on the contrary, the admonition is meekly accepted, and the pilot begins at once to gain confidence in himself. Daily he picks up more and more theoretical knowledge ; he notes what a coach may say of this or that man's faults, and he soon begins to see when certain admonitions are required. ·At least he can play the parrot, and can echo the coach's remarks when the mentor is absent, and before long he will have picked up enough to be able to discern when such a reproof is relevant and when it is not. In his spare time he often paddles a boat about on his own account, and this practice materially assists him in understanding the doctrines which he has to preach. As a rule, coxswains row in very good form, when they row at all ; and before their career closes many of them, though they have never rowed in a race, can teach much more of the science of oarsmanship than many a winning oar of a University race or of a Grand Challenge Cup contest.

A coxswain is the lightest item in the crew, but unless he sits properly he can do much harm in disturbing the balance of a light boat. He should sit with a straight back; if he slouches, he has not the necessary play of the loins to adapt himself to a roll of the boat. He should incline just a trifle forward; the spring of the boat at each stroke will swing him forward slightly, and he will recoil to an equal extent on the recovery. His legs should be crossed under him, like a tailor on a shop-board, with the outside of each instep resting on the floor of the boat. He should hold his rudder-lines just tight enough to feel the rudder. If he hangs too much weight upon them, he may jam the tiller upon the pin on which it revolves, so that, when the rudder has been put on and then taken off, the helm does not instantly swing back to the exact *status quo ante*; and in that case the calculation as to course may be disturbed, and a counter pull from the other line become necessary, in order to rectify the course.

A coxswain will do best to rest his hand lightly on either gunwale, just opposite to his hips. He should give the lines a turn round his palms, to steady the hold on them. Many coxswains tie a loop at the required distance, and slip the thumb through it; but such a loop should not be knotted too tight, for when rudder-lines get wet they shrink; so that a loop which was properly adjusted when the line was dry will be too far behind in event of the strings becoming soaked.

When a coxswain desires to set a crew in motion, the usual formula is to tell the men to 'get forward,' then to ask if they are 'ready,' and then to say 'go,' 'row,' or 'paddle,' as the case may be. When he wishes to stop the rowing, without otherwise to check the pace of the boat, the freshwater formula is 'easy all,' at which command the oars are laid flat on the water. In the navy the equivalent term is 'way enough.' 'Easy all' should be commanded at the beginning, or at latest at the middle, of a stroke, otherwise it is difficult for the men to stop all together and to avoid a half-commencement of the next stroke.

If a boat has to be suddenly checked and her way stopped, the order is ' Hold her all.' The blades are then slightly inclined towards the bow of the boat, causing them to bury in the water, and at the same time not to present a square surface to back-water. The handle of the oar should then be elevated, and more and more so as the decreasing way enables each oarsman to offer more surface resistance to the water. So soon as the way of the boat has been sufficiently checked, she can be backed or turned, according to what may be necessary in the situation.

In turning a long racing-boat care should be taken to do so gently, otherwise she may be strained. If there is plenty of room, she can be turned by one side of oars ' holding' her, while bow, and afterwards No. 3 also, paddle her gently round. If there is not room for a wide turn, then stroke and No. 6 should back water gently, against bow, &c. paddling.

A coxswain, when he first begins his trade, is pleased to find how obedient his craft is to the touch of his hand ; he pulls one string and her head turns that way ; he takes a tug at the other line, and she reverses her direction. The ease with which he can by main force bring her, somehow or other, to the side of the river on which he desires to be tends at first to make him overlook how much extra distance he unnecessarily covers by rough-and-ready hauling at the lines. ' Argonaut' [1] very lucidly uses the expression 'a boat should be *coaxed* by its rudder,' a maxim which all pilots will do well to make a cardinal point in their creed.

When a boat is once pointing in a required direction, and her true course is for the moment a straight one, the pilot should note some landmark, and endeavour to regulate his bows by aid of it, keeping the mark dead ahead, or so much to the right or to the left as occasion may require. In so doing he should feel his lines, and, so to speak, ' balance ' his bows on his *point d'appui*. His action should be somewhat analogous to what the play of his hand would be if he were attempting to

[1] Mr. E. D. Brickwood.

carry a stick end upwards on the tip of his finger. He would quickly but gently anticipate the declination denoted by each wavering motion of the stick, checking each such deviation the moment it is felt. In like manner when steering he should, as it were, 'hold' his bows on to his steering point, regulating his boat by gentle and timely touches; if he allows a wide deviation to occur, before he begins to correct his course, he has then a wide *détour* to make before he can regain his lost position. All this means waste of distance and of rowing energy on the part of the crew.

In steering by a distant landmark the coxswain must bear in mind that the parallax of the distant mark increases as he nears it ; so that what may point a true course to him, for all intents and purposes, when it is half a mile away, may lead him too much to one side or other if he clings to it too long without observing its altered bearing upon his desired direction.

When a coxswain has steered a course more than once he begins to know his landmarks and their bearing upon each part of the course. There is less strain upon his mind, and he becomes able to observe greater accuracy. There is nothing like having the 'eye well in' for any scene of action. A man plays relatively better upon a billiard-table or lawn-tennis ground to which he is well accustomed than on one to which he is a stranger ; and a jockey rides a horse all the better for having crossed him before the day of a race. However good a coxswain may be, he will steer a course more accurately, on the average, in proportion as he knows it more or less mechanically.

There is also a good deal in knowing the boat which has to be steered. No two ships steer exactly alike. Some come round more easily than others ; some fetch up into the wind more freely than others. In modern times it has been a common practice for builders to affix a movable 'fin' of metal to the bottom of a racing eight or four, under the after canvas, which fin can be taken out or fixed in at option. In a cross wind this helps to steady the track of a boat ; but, unless wind is strong and is abeam for a good moiety of the distance, the draw of the water all the way occasioned by the fin costs more than the extra drag of rudder which it obviates for just one part of the course.

In steering round a corner a coxswain should bear in mind that he must not expect to see his boat pointing in the direction to which he desires to make. His boat is a tangent to a curve, the curve being the shore. His bows will be pointing to the shore which he is avoiding. It is the position of his midship to the shore which he is rounding that he should especially note. The boat should be brought round as gradually as the severity of the wave will allow. If the curve is very sharp, like the corners of the 'Gut' at Oxford, or 'Grassy' or Ditton corners at Cambridge, the inside oars should be told to row light for a stroke or two. It will ease their labour, and also that of the oars on the other side.

When there is a stiff beam wind the bows of a racing craft tend to bear up into the wind's eye. The vessel is making leeway all the time ; therefore if the coxswain on such an occasion steers by a landmark which would guide him were the water calm, he will before long find himself much to leeward of where he should be. In order to maintain his desired course he should humour his boat, and allow her bow to hold up somewhat into the wind (to windward of the landmark which otherwise would be guiding him). To what extent he should do so he must judge for himself, according to circumstances and to his own knowledge of the leeward propensities of his boat. To lay down a hard-and-fast rule on this point would be as much out of place as to attempt to frame a scale of allowance which a Wimbledon rifleman ought to make for mirage or crosswind, when taking aim at a distant bull's-eye.

Generally speaking a coxswain should hug the shore when going against tide or stream, and should keep in mid-stream when going with it. (Mid-stream does not necessarily imply mid-river.) Over the Henley course, until 1886, a coxwain on the Berks side used to make for the shelter of the bank below Poplar Point, where the stream ran with less force. The alteration (for good) of the Henley course which was inaugurated in 1886 has put an end to this, and both racing crews now take a mid-stream course. The course is to all intents and purposes straight, and yet it will not do to keep the bows fixed on one point from start to finish. There is just a fraction of curve to the left in it, but so slight that one finger's touch of a line will deflect a boat to the full extent required. The church tower offers a landmark by which all pilots can steer, keeping it more or less to the right hand of the bows, and allowing for the increase of its parallax as the boat nears her goal.

Over the Putney water the best course has changed considerably during the writer's personal recollections. Twenty years ago the point entering to Horse Reach, and opposite to Chiswick Church, could be taken close. The Conservancy dredged the bed of the river, and also filled up a bight on the Surrey shore. This transferred the channel and the strongest current to the Middlesex side. In 1866 a head wind (against flood tide) off Chiswick raised the higher surf near to the towpath, showing that the main stream flowed there. It now runs much nearer to the Eyot.

Also the removal of the centre arch of old Putney Bridge drew the main flood tide more into mid-river than of old; and since then the new bridge has been built and the old one altogether removed, still further affecting the current in the same direction. There is a noticeable tendency in the present day, on the part of all pilots, whether in sculling matches or in eight-oar races, to take Craven Point too wide and to bear off into the bay opposite, on the Surrey shore. The course should be kept rather more mid-stream than of old, up to Craven steps, but the point should be taken reasonably close when rounding; there should not be, as has often been seen during the last six years, room for a couple more boats to race between the one on the Fulham side and the Craven bank.

In old days, when Craven Point used to be taken close, and when the set of the tide lay nearer to it than now, there ensued an important piece of pilotage called 'making the shoot.' It consisted in gradually sloping across the river, so as to take the Soapworks Point at a tangent, and thence to make for the Surrey arch of Hammersmith Bridge. This 'shoot' is now out of place : firstly, because the tide up the first reach from the start of itself now tends to bring the boat more into mid-river off the Grass Wharf and Walden's Wharf ; secondly, because the Soapworks Point should now be taken *wide*, and not close. The reason for this latter injunction is that the races of to-day, by agreement, go through the centre arch of Hammersmith Bridge. Now the flood tide does not run through the bridge at right angles to the span. It is working hard across to the Surrey shore. Therefore, if a boat hugs Soapworks Point as of old, and as if the course lay through the shore arch, that boat will have to come out, *across* tide, at an angle of about 25° to the set of the tide, in order to fetch the outer arch and to clear the buttress and the steamboat pier. Year after year the same blunder is seen. Pilots, of sculling boats and of eight-oars alike, wander away to the Surrey bay off Craven ; then they hug the shore till they reach the Soapworks foot-bridge, and then they have to cross half the tide on their right before they can safely point for the outer arch of the Suspension Bridge. A pilot should endeavour to keep in mid-river off Rosebank and the Crab Tree, and after passing the latter point he will, while pointing his bows well to the right of the arch which he intends to pass under, find the river move to the left under him, until, with little or no use of rudder, he finds himself in front of his required arch just as he reaches the bridge.

After passing the bridge a boat should keep straight on for another two hundred yards, else it will get into dead water caused by the eddy of the Surrey pier. At Chiswick the course may be taken wide (save and except, as in all cases, where force of wind alters circumstances). The main tide runs nearest to Chiswick Eyot. Horse Reach should be entered in mid-river ; there is little or no tide on the Surrey point below it.

Making for Barnes Bridge, the boat should keep fairly near to the Middlesex shore—how near depends upon whether the race is ordained to pass through the centre or the Middlesex arch of Barnes Bridge. Once through Barnes Bridge, the course should sheer in (if the centre arch has been taken) until the boat lies as if it had taken the shore arch. It should attain this position by the time it breasts the 'White Hart.' The river is here a horseshoe to the finish. In linear measure a boat on the Middlesex side has nearly two lengths less to travel than the one outside it between Barnes Bridge and the 'Ship.' The tide runs nearly as well within sixty feet of the shore as in mid-river at this point, hence it pays to keep about that distance from the Middlesex bank.

The old Thames watermen who instruct young pilots over the Putney course are often inclined to run too much in the grooves which were good in their younger days, when they themselves were racing on the river. Their instruction would be sound enough if the features of the river had not undergone change, as aforesaid, in sundry details. The repeated blunders of navigation lately seen perpetrated by watermen as well as amateurs between Craven Steps and Hammersmith make us lose much faith in watermen's tuition for steering the metropolitan course. We would rather entrust a young pilot to some active member of the London or Thames Rowing Clubs. These gentlemen know the river well enough as it now is, and are not biassed by old memories of what it once was but is no longer.

University coxswains have easier tasks in these days than their predecessors before 1868. Until the Thames Conservancy obtained statutory powers in 1868 to clear the course for boat-racing, it used to be a ticklish matter to pick a safe course on a flood tide. There would be strings of barges towed, and many more sailing, others 'sweeping,' up river. Traffic did not stop for sport. Coxswains often found themselves in awkward predicaments to avoid such itinerant craft, more so when barges were under sail against a head wind, and were tacking from shore to shore. In 1866 a barge of this sort most seriously interfered with the Cambridge crew in Horse Reach, just when Oxford had, after a stern race, given them the go-by off the

Bathing-place. It extinguished any chance which might have been left for Cambridge.

In the preceding year C. R. W. Tottenham immortalised himself by a great *coup* with a barge. She was tacking right across his course (Oxford had just gone ahead after having been led by a clear length through Hammersmith Bridge). This was just below Barnes Bridge. Many a pilot would have tried to go round the bows of that barge. At the moment when she shaped her course to tack across tide there seemed to be ample room to pass in front of her. Tottenham never altered his course, and trusted to his own calculations. Presently the barge was broadside on to Oxford's bows, and only a few lengths ahead. Every one in the steamers astern stood aghast at what seemed to be an inevitable smash. The barge held on, and so did Oxford, and the barge passed clear away just before Oxford came up. Even if she had hung a little, in a lull of wind, it would have been easy for Oxford to deflect a trifle and pass under her stern. Anything was better than attempting to go round her bows, which at first seemed to be the simplest course to spectators not experts at pilotage. It must be admitted that so much nerve and judgment at a pinch have never before or since been displayed by any coxswain in a University match. Tottenham had his opportunity and made the most of it. He steered thrice afterwards, but even if he had never steered again he had made his reputation by this one *coup*. In justice to other crack coxswains, such as Shadwell and Egan of old, and, *par excellence*, G. L. Davis in the present day, we must assume that if they had been similarly tried they would have been equally triumphant.

FOUR-OARS.

THE fewer the number of performers in a boat the longer does it take (with material of uniform quality) to acquire absolute evenness of action. This may seem paradoxical, but none the less all practical oarsmen will, from their own personal experiences, endorse the statement. It has been said that it takes twice as long to perfect a four as an eight, twice as long to perfect a pair as a four, and twice as long to perfect a sculler as a pair. This scale may be fanciful, but it is approximately truthful ; it refers, of course, to the education of oarsmen for work in the respective craft, from their earliest days of instruction. It means that a higher standard of watermanship has to be attained, in order to do justice to the style of craft rowed in, according as the ship carries more or fewer performers. Many an oarsman who by honest tugging can improve the go of an eight-oar will do more harm than good in a light four, and will be simply helpless in a racing pair.

Four-oar races, with the exception of some junior contests, are now rowed in coxswainless craft. The first of these seen in Europe was that of the St. John's Canadian crew (professional, but admitted for the nonce as amateurs) at the Paris International Regatta 1867. All the other crews carried steerers. The Canadians had the windward station in a stiff wind, and won easily. Next year the B.N.C. Oxon Club produced a four thus constructed at Henley. The rules did not forbid this ; but the novelty scared other competitors and threatened to spoil the racing in that class. The stewards accordingly passed a resolution forbidding any of the entries to dispense with a coxswain, and under cover of this disqualified the B.N.C. four when it came in ahead.

Next year the resolution referred to remained in force (as regards the Challenge Cups), but a presentation prize for fours without coxswains was given, and was won by the Oxford Bodleian Club. In 1871 the chief professional matches were rowed without coxswains ; but no more prizes were given for this class of rowing at Henley until 1873, when the Stewards' Cup was classed for 'no coxswains.' At Oxford college fours were similarly altered, but the steering was so bad that it was seriously proposed to revert to the old system. A similar proposal was made with regard to Henley. Fortunately, wiser counsels prevailed, and oarsmen realised that it was better to attempt to raise their own talents to the standard required for the improved build than to detract from the build to suit the failings of mediocrity. In 1875 the Visitors and Wyfold Cups were emancipated from coxswains, and since then the standard of amateur four-oar rowing has gradually risen to the requirements of the improved class of build.

Steerage is of course the main difficulty in these pairs. Three different sorts of apparatus have been used in them. Two of these are much of the same sort. One, generally in use to this day, consists of two bars projecting from the stretcher, and

44

working horizontally in slits cut in the board. The foot presses against one bar or other to direct the rudder. Another process is to fix a shoe to the stretcher, in which the oarsman places his foot. This shoe works laterally. The third is one tried by the writer in 1868. Every inventor thinks his goose a swan, and possibly the writer is over-sanguine as to the merits of his own hobby. It consists of two bars laid on the stretcher, like a very widely opened letter V, the arms of the V pointing in the direction of the sitter. Each arm is hinged at the apex of the V. The stretcher is grooved, so that either arm can be pressed into the groove, flush with the surface of the stretcher. Behind each bar is a spring. The bars cross the stretcher just about the ball of the foot. The hinge is sunk deep in the wood, so that the arms of the levers do not begin to project above the wood till some 5 inches on either side of the centre of the stretcher. The feet are placed in ordinary rowing pose, in the middle of the V, where the levers lie below the flush surface of the stretcher. The strap, though tight, has a *wide* loop, to admit of slight lateral movement of the feet. To put on rudder either foot is slipped half an inch or so outward. This brings it on to the lever of that side, and the pressure of the foot drives the lever flush. This pressure and movement of the lever, by means of another small lever and swivel outside the gunwale, in connection with it, works the rudder line. When steerage enough has been obtained, a half-inch return of the foot to its normal pose releases the lever, and the spring behind it at once brings it to *status quo ante*.

Now in the other two mechanisms above cited, the same foot has to steer *both* ways. Hence, for one of the two directions, the toe must turn in like a pigeon's. This must, for the moment, cripple leg-work, especially on slides. Again, with lateral movement in first and second machines, it is difficult for the steerer to know to exactness when his rudder is ' off.' He may, in returning it after steerage, leave it a trifle on, or carry it the other way too far. If so, he has to counter-steer a stroke or two later, till he feels that his rudder is free and trailing.

The writer claims for his own invention that it never removes the feet from the proper outward-turned pose against the stretcher, and that the springs under the lever ensure the rudder swinging back and 'trailing' so soon as a lever is released.

Whatever apparatus is used, *wires*, not strings, should lead the rudder, and should not be too tight ; they will pull enough, though slightly loose.

Anyone may steer ; the best waterman, if not too short-sighted, should do so, but stroke should not take the task if anyone else is at all fit for it.

FOUR-OAR.

The steerer should not be repeatedly looking round, as regards his course. If he is sure of no obstacles lying in his path, he can, when once he has laid his boat straight for a reach, watch her stern-post, and keep touch on it, to hold it to some landmark.

A coxswainless four really facilitates oarsmanship. It recovers from a roll more freely than the old-fashioned build with a pilot. It is uneven rowing which causes a roll, but when once equilibrium has been disturbed the coxswain has more difficulty than the crew in regaining balance. The oarsmen aid themselves with their oars, as with balancing poles. The removal of the coxswain therefore tends to reduce the rolling, and facilitates the speedy return of the ship to her keel when momentarily thrown off it. Coxswainless fours at Henley travel now much more steadily than did those with coxswains fifteen years ago. A runner on the bank, to look out for obstructive craft, is useful in practice. It enables the steerer to keep his eyes on his stern-post, and to guide his course thereby in confidence, without repeated twists round to see if any loafing duffer is going to smash his timbers. The pace of a first-class coxswainless four, in smooth water, for half a mile is quite as great as that of a second-class eight-oar with a coxswain. The abolition of coxswain has improved the speed of fours some forty seconds over the Henley course.

One good resulted from the attempt of B.N.C. in 1868 to row without a coxswain. It opened the eyes of the regatta executive to the unfairness of tolerating boy coxswains. The University clubs used to carry boys of four or five stone. In that very year the 'Oscillators' had a four-stone lad, while University College carried an eight-stone man. There was just as much difference between these two fours in dead weight carried as between B.N.C. (with no coxswain) and the Oscillators. University clubs are *ex officio* debarred from obtaining boys to steer. This inequality had been complained of by college crews time after time. Old Mr. Lane, the usual vice-chairman, used to sneer at the complaint, and say, 'If a boy can do in one boat what it takes a man to do in another, it is not fair to prohibit the boy.' If this were logical, then, *pari passu*, there could be no unfairness for one man to do single-handed what in other boats it took a man and a boy (or two men) to do, viz. both row and steer. Mr. Lane's fallacy was exploded by this *reductio ad absurdum* of his tenets, and regulation weights for coxswains were initiated for following years.

MORE than one master of oarsmanship has declared that good pair-oar rowing is the acme of oarsmanship. Just as there are fewer oarsmen who can do justice to a four-oar than to an eight, so when we come to pair-oars we find still fewer performers who can really show first-class style in this line of rowing. Much as watermanship is needed in a four, it is still more important to possess it when rowing in a pair. One, or even two men, out of a four-oared crew may be what would be considered bad watermen, i.e. not *au fait* at sitting a rolling boat, and not instinctively time-keepers. Yet, if the other two men have the quality of watermanship, the four may speedily fall together, provided the two outsiders show sound general principles of style. In a pair-oar, if either of the hands is a bad waterman, the combination will never rise above mediocrity. In pair-oar rowing there is needed a *je-ne-sais-quoi* sort of mutual concession of style. One man is stroke and the other bow, but there is in good pair-oarsmen an indefinite and almost unconscious give-and-take action on the part of both men. The style of the two is a sort of blend.

Old Harry Clasper, when asked which steered, of himself and his son Jack, in a pair, said that 'both steered.' To do this is the acme of homogeneous rowing. Of two partners one may, and should, act as chief ; but his colleague should be co-operating with him, and almost anticipating his motions and orders.

When two strange partners commence work, they should make up their minds not to row 'jealous.' If each begins by trying to row the other round, they will disagree like Richard Penlake and his wife. They had better each try to see who can do least work : sit the boat, paddle gently, studying to drop into the water together, to catch the water together, to finish together, to feather together (and cleanly), and to recover together. The less work they try to do, while thus seeking to assimilate their motions to each other, the quicker will they settle down.

As to rowing each other round, such emulation should never enter their heads. To row a partner round is no proof of having done more work than he towards propelling the boat. One man may catch sharply and row cleanly, and in a style calculated to make a boat travel ; his colleague may slither the beginning and tug at the end, staying a fraction of a second later in the water than the other, but rowing no longer in reach. The latter will probably row the boat round ! A tug at the end of a stroke turns a boat much more than a catch at the beginning ; yet the latter propels the racing boat far more. Of course, if two men row alike in style and reach from end to end, and one puts on all through the stroke a trifle more pressure, the ship will turn from the greater pressure. But, unless it can be guaranteed that the style of each partner is identical all through the stroke, 'rowing round' does not prove a superiority of work.

PAIR OARS—AN IMMINENT FOUL

We have said that good watermen will sit a pair where bad ones will roll. So far so good. But good watermen, first beginning practice with each other, must not assume that because they do not roll their uniformity is therefore proved. Their power of balance can keep the boat upright, even though there may be at first some inaccuracies of work. Thus to balance a boat requires a certain amount of exertion ; in a race, at this stage, this labour of balancing would take something off the power of the stroke. Besides, until the two oars work with similar pressure through the whole stroke, the keel cannot be travelling dead straight. Steady though good men may be at scratch, they will gain in pace as they continue to practise, and insensibly assimilate their action. With bad watermen cessation of rolling is a sign that the styles have at last assimilated ; with good watermen the deduction is not necessarily sound.

In old days pair-oars rowed without rudders. The two oars guided the ship. It was best to let the stronger man steer. He could thus set his partner to do his best all the way in a race, could ease an over or two, or lay on that much extra, from stroke to stroke, according as the stern-post required balancing on the landmark which had been selected as its *point d'appui*. To learn each other's strength and to know the course, to know by heart when to lay on for this corner, or to row off for that, was the study of practice and tested watermanship. In modern times a thin metal rudder is usually used, steered as in coxswainless fours. In a beam wind this materially aids pace, it enables the leeward oar to do his full share, instead of paddling while his partner is toiling. Even in still water it is some gain, provided the helm can be easily 'trailed' when not wanted. The facility with which such a pair can be steered tempts men to omit to study that delicate balance of a boat's stern on its point which was the acme of art before rudders came in. We have seen a (rudderless) pair leave a wake up Henley reach, from island to point, on a glassy evening, as straight as if a surveyor's line had been stretched there. In fact, to steer such a pair, with a practical partner, was, if anything, easier to some men than to steer an eight. The stern-post lay in view of the oarsman, and could be adjusted on its point like a gun barrel, whereas the actual bows of an eight are unseen by a coxswain.

Except a sculling boat, a pair-oar is the fastest starting of all craft; but if it is thus easy to set in motion at the outset of a race, it is plain that it can be spurted later on as suddenly. Bearing this in mind, there is no object in starting a pair in a race at a speed which cannot go all the way. There is as much scope for staying in a pair as in an eight; more in fact, for the pair takes the longer to do the same distance as the eight. The start should be quick, but it is best to keep a stroke or two per minute in hand for a rush hereafter, if needed, when the pulse of the enemy has been felt, and when partners have warmed to their work.

Pairs are best rowed with oars somewhat smaller all round than those which are used for eights or fours. The pair, more than any other craft, requires to be caught sharp and light; an oar that is not too long in the shank nor too big in the blade best accomplishes this. 'Dimensions' recommended for 'work' in various craft will be found scheduled elsewhere in this volume.

To conclude the subject of pairs, it may be added, if partners wish to assimilate, they must make up their minds to avoid recrimination. If the boat goes amiss say, or assume, 'it is I,' not 'you,' who is to blame. Keep cool and keep your head in a race. If the steersman bids 'easy' half a stroke, be prompt in so doing. To delay to right the course at the correct instant may take the ship lengths out of her course. A stroke eased in time, like a stitch, often saves nine, and perhaps obviates sticking in the bank.

SCULLING.

SCULLING needs more precision and more watermanship than rowing. The strongest man only wastes his strength in sculling if he fails to obtain even work for each hand. A pair-oar requires more practice to bring it to perfection than any other boat manned by oars, but a sculler requires considerably more practice than any pair of oarsmen. Strength he must have in proportion to his weight, if he is to soar above mediocrity, but strength alone will not avail him unless he gets his hands well together.

His sculls will overlap more or less. It is practically immaterial which hand he rows uppermost ; the upper hand has a trifle of advantage, and for this reason Oxonians, whose course is a left-hand one, usually scull left hand over. The first difficulty which an embryo sculler has to contend with is that of attaining uniform pressure with square body and square legs upon a pair of arms which are not uniformly placed. One arm has to give way to another to enable the hands to clear each other when they cross ; and yet while they do this the blades which they control should be buried to a uniform depth. How to attain this give-and-take action of the arms is better shown by even a moderate performer in five minutes of practical illustration than by reams of book instruction.

The aspirant to sculling honours had better, when commencing to learn, take his first lesson in a gig. A wager boat will be too unsteady, and will retard his practice ; ' skiffs ' are usually to be obtained only as teach boats with work at sixes and sevens. A dingey buries too much on the stroke, and spoils style. The beginner should find a stiff pair of sculls, true made, and overlapping about the width of his hands. He should ask some proficient to examine and to try his sculls, and to tell him by the feel whether they are really a pair. The best makers of oars and sculls too often turn out sculls which are not ' pairs,' and when this is the case the action of him who uses them cannot be expected to be even on both sides of his frame. Having got suitable sculls, let the sculler arrange his stretcher just a shade shorter than he would have it for rowing. He can clear his knees with a shorter stretcher when sculling than when rowing, as he can easily see for himself. A stretcher should always be as short as is compatible with clearing the knees.

Whether or not the pupil is proficient in sliding, he had better keep a fixed seat while learning the rudiments of sculling ; it will give him less to think about ; he might unconsciously contract faults in sliding while fixing his mind elsewhere—in the direction of his new implements.

He should see that his rowlocks are roomy. In most gigs there is a want of room between thowl and stopper. A sculler requires a wider rowlock than an oarsman, because his scull goes forward to an acuter angle than an oar, with the same reach of body. Nothing puts out a sculler's hands more than a recoil of the scull from the stopper, for want of room to reach out. The sculler should examine whether his rowlocks are true ; the sills of them should be horizontal, not inclined, and most of all not inclined from stern to bow ; the latter defect will at once make him scull deep. Next, let him examine his thowl. This should be clean faced, not 'grooved' by the upper edge of the loom of oars which have been handled by operators who feather under water, and who thus force at the finish with the upper edge and not with the flat back of the loom. Half the hack gigs that are on hire will be found to have rowlocks so worn, grooved, and disfigured, that not the best sculler in the world can lay his strength out on them until he has filed them into shape. The thowl should show a flush surface, and rake just the smallest trifle aft, so as to hold the blade just a fraction of an angle less than a rectangle to the water, but this 'rake' should be very slight.

Having now got his tools correct, the workman will have no excuse for grumbling at them if he fails to do well. Let him begin by paddling gently and slowly. He had better not attempt to work hard. If he sees some other sculler shooting past him in a similar boat, he must sink all jealousy. Every motion which he makes in a stroke is now laying the foundation of habit and of mechanical action hereafter ; hence he must give his whole mind to each stroke, and be content to go to work steadily and carefully. He must feel his feet against his stretcher, both legs pressing evenly. He must hold his sculls in his fingers (not his fists), and let the top joint of each thumb cap the scull. This is better than bringing the thumb under the scull ; it gives the wrists more play, and tends to avoid cramp of the forearm. He must endeavour to do his main work with his body and legs, when he has laid hold of the water. He should keep his arms rigid, and lean well back. Just as he passes the perpendicular his hands will begin to cross each other. Whichever hand he prefers to row over, he should stick to. When the hands begin to cross, he should still try to keep the arms stiff, and to clear the way by slightly lowering one hand and raising the other. Not until his hands have opened out again after having crossed should he begin to bend his arms and to bring the stroke home to the chest. He should try to bend each arm simultaneously and to the same extent, and to bring each hand up to his breast almost at his ribs, at equal elevations. He must try to feather both sculls sharply and simultaneously.

If he finds any difficulty in this, he will do well to give himself a private lesson on this point before he proceeds further. He can sit still and lay his sculls in the rowlocks, and thus practise turning the wrists sharply, on and off the feather, till he begins to feel more handy in this motion.

On the recovery he should shoot his hands out briskly, the body following but not waiting for the hands to extend—just as in a 'rowing' recovery. When the recovering hands begin to cross each other the lower and upper must respectively give way, and so soon as they open out after the cross, they should once more resume the same plane, and extend equally, so as to be ready to grip the water simultaneously for the succeeding stroke.

Very few scullers realise the great importance of even action of wrists. If one scull hangs in the water a fraction of a second more than another, or buries deeper, or skims lighter, the two hands at that moment are not working evenly. Therefore the boat is not travelling in a straight line ; therefore she will sooner or later, may be in the latter half of the very same stroke, have to be brought back to her course. In order to bring her back, the hand which, earlier, was doing the greater work, must now do less. Therefore the boat has not only performed a zigzag during the stroke, but also she has been, while so meandering, propelled by less than her full available forces, first one hand falling off through clumsiness, and afterwards the other hand shutting off some work, in order to equalise matters.

As the sculler becomes more used to his action, he will find his boat keep more even. At first he will be repeatedly putting more force on one hand than on another, and will have to rectify his course by counterwork with the neglected hand. Some scullers, though otherwise good, never steer well. They do not watch their stern-post, to see if they go evenly at each stroke ; still less, if they see a slight deflection to one hand after one stroke, do they at once rectify the deviation by extra pressure on the other hand during the ensuing stroke. A good steerer in sculling will correct his course even to half a stroke ; if through a bend, or a wave, or other cause, he sees one hand has taken the other a little round by the time that the sculls are crossing, he will row the other hand home a trifle sharper, and so bring the keel straight by the time he feathers. When a sculler gets more settled to his work, and has got over the first difficulty of clearing his hands at the crossing, he will begin to acquire the knack of bringing the boat round to one hand, without any distinct extra tug of that scull. He will press a trifle more with the one foot, and will throw a little more of his weight on to the one scull, and so produce the desired effect on his boat.

When a sculler promotes himself to a light boat, he must be very careful not to lose the knack of even turns of wrists which he has been so assiduously studying in his tub. In the wager boat, far more than in the tub, is the action of the sculler's body affected and his labour crippled by any uneven action of either hand. The gig did not roll if one hand went into the water an infinitesimal fraction of a second sooner, or came out that much later than the other hand. But the fragile sculling boat, with no keel, and about thirteen inches of beam, resents these liberties, and requires ' sitting ' in addition, whenever any inequality of work takes her off her balance. The sculler must especially guard against feathering under water. He is more tempted to do so now, while he is in an unsteady boat, than when he was in his sober-going gig. He feels instinctively that if he lets his blades rest flat on the water for

K 2

57

the instant, when his stroke concludes, he obtains for the moment a rectification of balance ; the flat blades stop rolling to either side ; when he has thus steadied his craft, then he can essay to lift his blades and to get forward. If he once yields to this insidious temptation, he runs the risk of spoiling himself as a sculler, and of ensuring that he will never rise beyond mediocrity. The hang back, and the sloppy feather, which are to be seen in so many second-class scullers, may almost invariably, if the history of the sculler be known, be traced to want of nerve and of confidence in early days to feather boldly, and to lift the sculls sharp from the water, regardless of rolling. Of course, for the nonce, the sculler can sit steadier, and therefore make more progress, if he thus steadies his craft with his blades momentarily flat ; and it is because of this fact that so many beginners are seduced into the trick. But let the sculler pluck up courage, and endeavour to imagine himself still afloat in his gig. Let him turn his wrists as sharply as when he was in her, and lift his blades boldly out, not even caring if he rolls clean over. There really is little chance of his so capsizing. If he rolls, his one blade or other floats in the water, and being strung over at the row-lock, cannot well let his boat turn over, so long as he holds on to the handle. Meantime, he must sit tight to his boat, and use his feet to balance her with his body. He must not try to row too fast a stroke ; a quick stroke hides faults, and speed tends to keep a light craft on an even keel so long as her crew are fresh ; but style is not learned while oarsmen or scullers are straining their utmost. If the sculler finds that he really cannot make progress in his wager boat, he must assume that he wants another spell of practice in his tub, and must revert again to her for a week or two, or more. If he will only persevere in studying even and simultaneous action of hands, he will get his reward in time.

He should not be ambitious to race too soon. Many a young sculler spoils himself by aspiring to junior scullers' races before he is ripe for racing. It is a temptation to have a ' flutter,' just to see how one gets on, but it is of no use to race unless the competitor has had some gallops beforehand ; and it is in trying to row a fast stroke before they can thoroughly sit a boat that so many scullers sow seeds of bad style, which stick to them long afterwards, and perhaps always. When at last the sculler has learned to sit his boat, to drop his hands in simultaneously, to feel an even pressure with both blades, to see his stern-post hold on true, and not waver from side to side ; when he is able to drop and turn both wrists at the same instant, to lift both blades clean away from the water, and to shoot out his hands without fouling either his knees or the water, then he has mastered more than half the scullers of the

A SPILL.

day—even though he can only perform thus for half-a-dozen strokes at a time without encountering a roll. He can now lay his weight well on his sculls, and can make his boat travel. He will have done well if all this time he has abstained from indulging in a slide ; he does not need one as yet, he is not racing, and the fewer things he has to think about the better chance he has of being able to devote his attention to acquiring even hands and a tight seat. Once let him gain these accomplishments, and he can then take to his slide, and in his first race go by many an opponent who started sculling long before him, but who began at once in a wager boat and on a slide.

A very good amateur sculler—J. E. Parker, winner of the Wingfield Sculls in 1863—used to say that he always went back until his sculls came out of the water of their own accord. As a piece of chaff, it used to be said of him, by his friends, that there was a greasy patch on his fore canvas, where his head came in contact with it at the end of his stroke. Of course this was only a jest, but undoubtedly Parker swung farther back than most scullers, perhaps more than any amateur. The secret of his pace, which was indisputable, as also his staying power, probably lay to a great extent in this long back swing of his. He also sculled exceedingly cleanly, his hands worked in perfect unison, and his blades came out clean and sharp. The writer cannot recall any sculler whose blades were so clean, save Hanlan and also W. S. Unwin in 1886. Much of the secret of each of these scullers lay in the evenness of their hands ; they wasted no power. F. Playford, junior, was a more powerful sculler, and apparently faster than either of the above-named amateurs (*ceteris paribus* as to slides, *quâ* Parker) ; but taking his reach and weight into consideration, it is not to be wondered if Playford was in his day the best of all Wingfield winners. The late Mr. Casamajor was a great sculler. He also had a very long back swing, and clean blades. He never had such tough opponents to beat as had Playford, but at least it could be said of him that he was unbeaten in public in any race.

Steerage apparatus is in these days fitted to many a sculling boat. The writer, as an old stager, is bound to admit that he had retired from active work before such mechanism was used, he therefore cannot speak practically as to its value for racing. So far as he has watched its use by scullers, he is induced to look upon the contrivance with suspicion. On a stormy day, with beam wind for a considerable part of the course, such an appendage will undoubtedly assist a sculler. It will save him from having an arm almost idle in his lap during heavy squalls. But on fairly smooth days, or when wind is simply ahead, a rudder must surely detract more from pace (by reason of the water which it catches, even when simply on the trail) than it ever will save by obviating the operation of rowing a boat round by the hand to direct her course. Again, the fittings which carry the rudder must, when the rudder is unshipped, hold a certain amount of water to the detriment of speed. Also, if a boat is pressed for a spurt, there must be some risk of the tiller of the rudder (however delicately made), and the wires which control it, pulling and drawing the water. When the canvas ducks under water on recovery, it is important that the water should run off freely when the boat springs to the stroke. If a post stands up at the stern, however thin and metallic, this must to some degree check the flow off of the water. Again, the feet must be moved to guide this rudder ; while they are thus shifting, the fullest power of the legs can hardly be applied. A sculler who is in good practice, and who is at home with his boat and sculls, should be able to feel his boat's course through each stroke, and to adjust her at any one stroke if she has deviated during the preceding one. On the whole, barring circumstances such as a stiff westerly wind at Henley, or a gale on the tideway course, scullers will do best without rudders ; and if a competitor desires to provide against the contingency of weather which will make a rudder advantageous, he had better, if he can, have a spare boat fitted for that purpose, so that if the water after all is smooth he will not be carrying any projecting metal at his stern to draw the water and to check his pace.

There is another objection to the use of rudders, especially for young scullers. It tempts them to rely on the rudder to rectify their course, instead of studying even play of hands so that the boat may have no excuse for deviating at all in smooth water.

All that has been said of the use of slides applies equally to sculling as to rowing. The leg action, as compared to swing, should be just the same when sculling as in rowing. That is, the slide should last as long as the swing. Now, in sculling, a man should go back much further than he does when rowing an oar. When he has an oar in his hand there is a limit to the distance to which he can spring back with good effect. His oar describes an arc ; when he has gone back beyond a certain distance the butt of his oar-handle will come at the middle of his breast or even more inside the boat. In such a position he cannot finish squarely and with good effect. Therefore he cannot go back *ad lib.* But the sculler is always placed evenly to his work, it is not on one side of him more than another. He should, when laying himself out for pace, swing back so far that his sculls come out just as his hands touch his ribs. In a wager boat, when well practised, he can afford to let his sculls overlap as much as six or even seven inches. But, after all, the extent of overlap is a matter of taste with so many scullers, that it would be unwise to lay down any hard and fast rule, beyond saying that at least the handles should overlap four inches, or, what is much the same, one hand should at least cover the other when the sculls lie in the rowlocks at right angles to the keel.

To return to the slide in sculling. Since the back swing should be longer in sculling than in rowing, and as there is a limit to the length which any pair of legs can slide, and since also it has been laid down as a rule that both when sculling and when rowing the slide should be economised so that it may last as long as the swing lasts, the reader will gather that the legs will have to extend more gradually when sliding to sculls than when sliding to oars. Therefore a man accustomed to row on slides, and whose legs are more or less habituated to a certain extension coupled with swing when rowing, must keep a watch upon himself when sculling lest his rowing habits should make him finish his slide prematurely, when he needs to prolong his swing for sculling. Unless his slide lasts out his swing, his finish, after legs have been extended, will only press the boat without propelling her.

In rowing an oarsman is guilty of fault if he meets or even pulls up to his oar. In sculling, with a very long swing back it is not a fault to commence the recovery of the body while the hands are still completing their journey home to the ribs. The body should not drop, nor slouch over the sculls while thus meeting them. It should recover with open chest and head well up, simply pulling itself up slightly, to start the back swing, by the handles of the sculls as they come home for the last three or four inches of their journey. Casamajor always recovered then, so did Hanlan, so did Parker, and any sculler who does likewise will sin (if he does sin in the opinion of some hypercritics of style) in first-class company. The fact is, this very long swing back (with straight arms) entails much recovery, and yet materially adds to pace. The sculler can afford to ease his recovery in return for the strain of his long stroke. Also lest his long swing should press the boat's bows, he can ease her recovery as well as his own, so soon as the main force of the long drag comes to an end. In the writer's opinion, unless a sculler really does go back *à la* Casamajor & Co. with straight arms and stiff back, and until his sculls come out of the water almost of their own accord as he brings his hands in, it is not an advantage for him to pull himself up to his handles to this trifling extent at the finish. A sculler who does not swing back further than when he is rowing, will do best to row his sculls home just as he would an oar.

In racing all men like a lead. If a sculler can take a lead with his longest stroke, swinging back as far as he can, and can feel that he is not doing a stroke too fast for his stamina, by all means let him do so ; but let him be careful not to hurry his stroke and thereby to shorten his back swing simply for the sake of a lead. Many a long-swing sculler spoils his style, at all events for the moment, by sprinting and trying to cut his opponent down. It is almost best for him if he finds that his opponent has the pace of him, and if he therefore relapses to his proper style, and bides his time. If he does so, he will go all the faster over the course for sticking to his style regardless of momentary lead. Some scullers lay out their work for pace, regardless of lasting power. When Chambers rowed Green in 1863, he tried to head the Australian, flurried himself, shortened his giant reach, lost pace, and, after all, lost the lead. When he realised that, force pace as much as he could, Green was too speedy, the Tyne man settled to his long sweep, and at once went all the faster, though now sculling a slower stroke.

It was not long before Green began to come back to him, and the result of that match is history.

Similarly, the writer recollects seeing the celebrated Casamajor win the Diamonds for the last time, in 1861. He was opposed by Messrs. G. R. Cox and E. D. Brickwood. Cox was a sculler who laid himself out for fast starting : he used very small blades, he did not swing further back than when rowing, and he sculled a very rapid stroke. He had led both Casamajor and H. Kelley in a friendly spin earlier in the year, and it was said that it was to vindicate his reputation as being still the best sculler of the day that the old unbeaten amateur once more entered for the Diamonds, where he knew he would encounter Cox in earnest, and no longer in play. (Casamajor was by no means in good health, and the grave closed over him in the following August.)

In the race in question Cox darted away with the lead. Casamajor had hitherto led all opponents in real racing, and *amour propre* seemed to prompt him to bid for the lead against the new flyer ; he quickened and quickened his stroke, till his long swing back vanished, and his boat danced up and down, but he could not hold Cox. Brickwood was last, rowing his own style, and sculling longest of the three. After passing the Farm gate, Casamajor suddenly changed his style, and went back to his old swing. Maybe, Cox had already begun to come to the end of his tether ; but, be that as it may, from the instant that Casamajor re-adopted his old swing back, he held Cox. (It did not look as if the pace was really falling off, for both the leaders were still drawing away from Brickwood.) In another minute Casamajor began to draw up to the leader, still swinging back as before. Then he went ahead, and all was over. Brickwood in the end rowed down Cox, and came in a good second. Casamajor at that time edited the ' Field ' aquatics. His own description therein of himself in the race seems to imply that he realised how he had at first thrown away his speed by bidding for the lead, and that he purposely, and not unconsciously, changed his style about the end of the first minute and a half of the race. His description of his own sculling at that juncture (modestly penned) was 'now rowing longer and with all his power.' This was quite true—he was not using his full power until he relapsed to his old style. These illustrations of two of the best scullers ever seen bidding for impossible leads, and then realising their mistakes in time, may be taken to heart by all modern and future aspirants to sculling honour.

SCULLING RACE, WITH PILOTS IN EIGHT-OARS.

Another reason why scullers like a lead is that it saves them from being 'washed' by a leader, and, conversely, enables them to 'wash an opponent.' In old days of boat-racing under the old code, lead was of importance, to save water being taken. Under new rules of boat-racing (which figure elsewhere in this volume), water can only be taken at peril. There is not, therefore, so much importance in lead as of old. As to 'wash,' if a man can sit a sculling boat, he does not care much for wash. Anyhow, he can, if in his own water, and if his adversary crosses him, steer exactly in his leader's wake ; the wash then spreads like a swallow's tail on either side of the sternmost man, and does not affect him. His opponent must get out of his way, if not overtaken, so he need not disturb himself ; and if the leader insists on steering to right or left simply to direct the wash, he loses more ground by this meandering than even the pursuer will lose by the slight perturbations of a sculling boat's wash for a few strokes. It is good practice for any sculler to take his boat now and then in the wake of another sculler, and try to 'bump' him. It will teach him how to sit his boat under such circumstances, and he will be surprised before long to find out how little he cares for being washed by another sculler.

A sculler, when practising over a course, especially when water is smooth, may with advantage time himself from day to day at various points of the course. He will thus find out what his best pace is, and will ascertain whether his speed materially falls off towards the end, if he forces extra pace at the start or halfway or so on. He must be careful to judge *proportionately* of times and distances, and not positively ; for streams may vary, and so may wind.

On the tideway in sculling matches, it is usual for pilots to conduct scullers. The pilot sits in the bow of an eight. The sculler may rely on the pilot to signal to him whether he is in the required direction ; but when he once knows that his boat points right, he should note where her stern points, just as if he were steering upon his own resources, and should endeavour so to regulate his hands that his stern keeps straight, as shown by some distant landmark which he selects. This straight line he should then maintain to the best of his ability, bringing his stern-post back to it, if it deflects, until his pilot again signals to him to change his course, for rounding some curve or for clearing some obstacle. The pilot cannot inform his charge of each small inaccuracy which leads eventually to deflection from the correct line ; this the sculler must provide against on his own account. It is only when the course has to be changed, or when the sculler has palpably gone out of his course, that the signals of the pilot come into play. Some scullers seem to make up their minds to leave everything to their pilots; the result is that their boats are never in a straight line; first they go astray to one side, and then, when signalled back, they take a stroll to the other side. Such scullers naturally handicap themselves greatly by thus losing ground through these tortuous wanderings. The simplest method of signalling by pilot is to hold a white handkerchief. In the right or left hand it means 'pull right or left,' respectively. When down, it means ' boat straight and keep it so.' If the pilot gets far astern, or if dangers are ahead which are beyond pilotage, taking off the hat means 'look out for yourself.'

When wind is abeam, a pilot cutter can materially aid a sculler by bringing its bow close on his windward quarter, thereby sheltering his stern from the action of the wind. Races such as that of Messrs. Lowndes and Payne for the Wingfield Sculls in 1880, when Mr. Payne did not row his opponent down until the last mile had well begun, should remind all scullers that a race is never lost till it is won, and that, however beaten you may feel, it is possible that your opponent feels even worse, and that he may show it in the next few strokes.

PUMPED OUT.

DIET.

THAT 'condition' tells in all contests, whether in brain labours such as chess matches or in athletics, is known to children in the schoolroom.

Training is the *régime* by means of which condition is attained. Its dogmas are of two orders : (1) Those which relate to exercise, (2) those which refer to diet. Diet of itself does not train a man for rowing or any other kind of athletics. What trains is hard work ; proper diet keeps the subject up to that work.

The effect of a course of training is twofold. It develops

those muscles which are in use for the exercise in question, and it also prepares the internal organs of heart and lungs for the extra strain which will be put upon them during the contest. All muscles tend to develop under exercise, and to dwindle under inaction. The right shoulder and arm of a nail-maker are often out of all proportion to the left ; the fingers of a pianist develop activity with practice, or lose it if the instrument be discontinued.

Training is a thorough science, and it is much better understood in these days than when the writer was in active work ; and again, the trainers of his day were in their turn far ahead of those of the early years of amateur oarsmanship. From the earliest recorded days of athletic contests, there seems to have been much faith pinned to beefsteaks. When Socrates rebukes Thrasymachus, in the opening pages of Plato's ' Republic,' he speaks of beefsteaks as being the chief subject of interest to Polydamos, who seems to have been a champion of the P.R. of Athens of those days. The beefsteak retains its prestige to the present day, but it is not the *ne plus ultra* which it was in 1830.

The earliest amateur crews seem to have rowed in many instances without undergoing a course of training and of reduction of fat. But when important matches began to be made, the value of condition was appreciated. Prizefighters had then practical training longer than any other branch of athletics, and it was by no means uncommon for watermen, when matched by their patrons, to be placed under the super-vision of some mentor from the P.R. as regards their diet and exercise. But before long watermen began to take care of themselves in this respect. Their system of training did not differ materially from that in vogue with the P.R. It consisted of hard work in thick clothing, early during the course of preparation, to reduce weight ; and a good deal of pedestrian exercise formed part of the day's programme ; a material result of the association of the P.R. system of preparation. The diet was less varied and liberal than in these days, but abstinence from fluid to as great an extent as possible was from the outset recognised as all-important for reducing bulk and clearing the wind.

A prizefighter or waterman used to commence his training with a liberal dose of physic. The idea seems to have a stable origin, analogous to the principle of physic balls for a hunter on being taken up from grass. The system was not amiss for men of mature years, who had probably been leading a life of self-indulgence since the time when they had last been in training. But when University crews began to put themselves under the care of professional trainers, those worthies used to treat these half-grown lads as they would some gin-sodden senior of forty, and would physic their insides before they set them to work. They would try to sweat them down to fiddle-strings, and were not happy unless they could show considerable reduction of weight in the scale, even with a lad who had not attained his full growth. Still, though many a young athlete naturally went amiss under this severe handling, there is no doubt that these professional trainers used to turn out their charges in very fine condition, on the average.

No trainer of horses would work a two-year-old on the same system that he would an aged horse ; and the error of these old professional trainers lay in their not realising the difference in age between University men and the ordinary classes of professional athletes. In time University men began to think and to act for themselves in the matter of training. When college eights first began to row against each other, there were only three or four clubs which manned eights ; and these eights now and then were filled up with a waterman or two. (In these days few college crews would take an Oxford water-man at a gift — *quâ* his oarsmanship !) These crews, when they began to adopt training, employed watermen as mentors. Before long there were more eights than watermen, and some crews could not obtain this assistance. The result was, a rule against employing professional tuition within a certain date of the race. This regulation threw University men upon their own resources, and before long they came to the conclusion that good amateur coaching and training was more effective than that of professionals. Mr. F. Menzies, the late Mr. G. Hughes, and the Rev. A. Shadwell, had much to do in converting the O.U.B.C. to these wholesome doctrines. From that time amateurs of all rowing clubs have very much depended on themselves and their *confrères* for tuition in oarsmanship and training.

The usual *régime* of amateur training is now very much to the following effect.

Réveille at 6.30 or 7 A.M.—Generally a brief morning walk ; and if so, the 'tub' is usually postponed until the return from the walk. If it is summer, and there are swimming facilities, a header or two does no harm, but men should not be allowed to strike out hard in swimming, when under hard rowing rules. For some reason, which medical science can better explain, there seems to be a risk of straining the suspensory or some other ligaments, when they are suddenly relaxed in water, and then extended by a jerk. (This refers to arms that have lately been bearing the strain of rowing.) Also, the soakage in water for any length of time tends to relax the whole of the muscular system. Whether tub or swim be the order of the morning, the skin should be well rubbed down with rough towels after the immersion. In old days there used to be a *furore* for running before breakfast. Many young men find their stomachs and appetites upset by hard work on an empty stomach, more especially in sultry weather. The Oxford U.B.C. eight at Henley in 1857 and 1859 used to go for a run up Remenham Hill before breakfast, and this within two or three days of the regatta. Such a system would now be tabooed as unsound.

Breakfast consists of grilled chops or steaks ; cold meat may be allowed if a man prefers it. If possible, it is well to let a roast joint cool *uncut*, to supply cold meat for a crew. The gravy is thus retained in the meat.

Bread should be one day old ; toast is better than bread. Many crews allow butter, but as a rule a man is better without it. It adds a trifle to adipose deposit, and does not do any special service towards strengthening his tissues or purifying his blood.

Some green meat at breakfast is a good thing. Watercress for choice—next best are small salad and lettuce (plain).

Tea is the recognised beverage ; two cups are ample for a man. If he can dispense with sugar it will save him some ounces of fat, if he is at all of a flesh-forming habit of body. A boiled egg is often allowed, to wind up the repast.

GOING TO SCALE.

Luncheon depends, as to its substance, very much upon the time of year and the hours of exercise. If the work can be done in two sections, forenoon and afternoon, all the better. In hot summer weather it may be too sultry to take men out between breakfast and the mid-day meal. Luncheon now usually consists of cold meat, to a reasonable amount, stale bread, green meat, and a glass of ale. In the days when the writer was at Oxford, the rule of the O.U.B.C. was to allow no meat at luncheon (only bread, butter, and watercress). This was a mistake; young men, daily wast'ng a large amount of tissue under hard work, had a natural craving for substantial food to supply the hiatus in the system. By being docked of it at luncheon, they gorged all the more at breakfast and dinner, where there was no limit as to quantity (of solids) to be consumed. They would have done better had their supply of animal food been divided into three instead of two daily allowances. They used to be allowed one slice of cold meat during their nine days' stay at Putney; it would have been well to have allowed this all through training.

Dinner consists mainly of roast beef or mutton, or choice of both. It is the custom to allow 'luxuries' of some sort every other day, e.g. fish one day, and a course of roast poultry (chicken) on another. 'Pudding' is sometimes allowed daily, sometimes it only appears in its turn with 'luxuries.' It generally consists of stewed fruit, with plain boiled rice, or else calves'-foot jelly. A crust, or biscuit, with a little butter and some watercress or lettuce, make a final course before the cloth is cleared.

Drink is ale, for a standard; light claret, with water, is nowadays allowed for choice, and no harm in it. A pint is the normal measure; sometimes an extra half-pint may be conceded on thirsty days.

An orange and biscuit for dessert usually follow. In the writer's days every man had two glasses of port wine. He thinks this was perhaps more than was required (as regards alcohol); one glass may suffice, but there may be no reason against the second wineglass being conceded, with water substituted, if the patient is really dry. Claret also may take the place of port after dinner. Fashions change; in the writer's active days, claret would have been scorned as un-English for athletes.

Such is the usual nature of training diet; of the exercise of the day, more anon. There does not seem to be much fault to find with the *régime* above sketched; in fact, the proof of soundness of the diet may be seen in the good condition usually displayed by those who adopt it.

All the same, the writer, when he has trained crews, has slightly modified the above in a few details. He has allowed (a little) fish or poultry daily, as an extra course, and for the same reason has always endeavoured to have both beef and mutton on the table. He believes that change of dish aids appetite, so long as the varieties of food do not clash in digestion. Men become tired with a monotony of food, however wholesome. Puddings the writer does not think much of, provided that other varieties of dish can be obtained. A certain amount of vegetable food is necessary to blend with the animal food, else boils are likely to break out ; but green vegetables such as are in season are far better than puddings for this purpose. Salad, daily *with the joint*, will do good. It is unusual to see it, that is all. The salad should not be dressed. Lettuce, endive, watercress, smallcress, beetroot, and some minced spring onions to flavour the whole, make a passable dish, which a hungry athlete will much relish. Asparagus, spinach, and French beans may be supplied when obtainable. Green peas are not so good, and broad beans worse. The tops of young nettles, when emerald green, make a capital dish, like spinach, rather more tasty than the latter vegetable. Such nettles can only be picked when they first shoot ; old nettles are as bad as flowered asparagus.

If a crew train in the fruit season, fruit to a small amount will not harm them, as a finale to either breakfast or dinner. But the fruit should be *very* fresh, not bruised nor decomposed ; strawberries, gooseberries, grapes, peaches, nectarines, apricots (say one of the last three, or a dozen of the smaller fruits, for a man's allowance), all are admissible. Not so melons, nor pines—so medical friends assert.

In hot summer weather it is as well to dine about 2 P.M., to row in the cool of the evening, towards 7 P.M., and to sup about 8.30 or 9 P.M. It is a mistake to assume that because a regatta will come off midday, therefore those who train for it should accustom themselves to a burning sun for practice. With all due deference to Herodotus (who avers that the skeleton skulls of quondam combatant Persians and Egyptians could be known apart on the battle-field, because the turban-clad heads of Persians produced soft skulls which crumbled to a kick, while the sun-baked heads of Egyptians were hard as bricks), we do not believe in this sort of acclimatisation. If men have to be trained to row a midnight race, they would be best prepared for it by working at their ordinary daylight hours, not by turning night into day for weeks beforehand. On the same principle it would seem to be a mistake to expose oarsmen in practice to excessive heat to which they have not been accustomed, solely because they are likely eventually to row their race under a similar sun. In really oppressive weather at Henley the writer and his crews used to dine about 2 P.M. as aforesaid, finish supper at 9 or 9.30, and go to bed two hours later. They rose proportionately later next day, taking a good nine hours in bed before they turned out. So far as their records read, those crews do not seem on the whole to have suffered in condition by this system of training.

Many men are parched with thirst at night. The heat of the stomach, rather overladen with food, tends to this. The waste of the system has been abnormal during the day ; the appetite, i.e. instinct to replenish the waste, has also been abnormal, and yet the capacity of the stomach is only normal. Hence the stomach finds it hard work to keep pace with the demands upon it. Next morning these men feel 'coppered,' as if they had drunk too much overnight, and yet it is needless to say they have not in any way exceeded the moderate scale of alcohol already propounded above as being customary.

The best preventive of this tendency to fevered mouths is a cup of 'water gruel,' or even a small slop-basin of it, the last thing before bedtime. It should not contain any milk ; millet seed and oatmeal grits are best for its composition. The consumption of this light supper should be *compulsory*, whether it suits palates or not. The effect of it is very striking ; it seems to soothe and promote digestion, and to allay thirst more than three times its amount of water would do. Some few men cannot, or profess to be unable to, stomach this gruel. The writer has had to deal with one or two such in his time. He had his doubts whether their stomach or their whims were to blame ; but in such cases he gave way, and allowed a cup of chocolate instead—*without milk.* (Milk blends badly with meat and wine at the end of a hard day.) Chocolate is rather more fattening than gruel, otherwise it answers the same purpose, of checking any disposition to 'coppers.'

It has been a time-honoured maxim with all trainers, that it is the fluids which lay on fat and which spoil the wind. Accordingly, reduction in the consumption of fluid has always been one of the first principles of training, and it is a sound one so long as it is not carried to excess. It is not at the outset of training that thirst so oppresses the patient, but at the end of the first week and afterwards, especially when temperature rises and days are sultry. Vinegar over greens at dinner tends to allay thirst ; the use of pepper rather promotes it. In time the oarsman begins to accustom himself somewhat to his diminished allowance of fluid, and he learns to economise it during his meals, to wash down his solids.

A coach should be reasonably firm in resisting unnecessary petitions for extra fluid, but he must exercise discretion, and need not be always obdurate. On this subject the writer reproduces his opinion as expressed in 'Oars and Sculls' in 1873 :—

The tendency to 'coppers' in training is no proof of insobriety. The whole system of training is unnatural to the body. It is an excess of nature. Regular exercise and plain food are not in themselves unnatural, but the amount of each taken by the subject in training is what is unnatural. The wear and tear of tissue is more than would go on at ordinary times, and consequently the body requires more commissariat than usual to replenish the system. The stomach has all its work cut out to supply the commissariat, and leave the tendency to indigestion and heat in the stomach. A cup of gruel seldom fails to set this to rights, and a glass of water besides may also be allowed if the coach is satisfied that a complaint of thirst is genuine. There is no greater folly than stinting a man in his liquid. He should not be allowed to blow himself out

M

with drink, taking up the room of good solid food ; but to go to the other extreme, and to spoil his appetite for want of an extra half-pint at dinner, or a glass of water at bedtime, is a relic of barbarism. The appetite is generally greatest about the end of the first week of training. By that time the frame has got sufficiently into trim to stand long spells of work at not too rapid a pace. The stomach has begun to accustom itself to the extra demands put upon it, and as at this time the daily waste and loss of flesh is greater than later on, when there is less flesh to lose, so the natural craving to replenish the waste of the day is greater than at a later period. At this time the thirst is great, and though drinking out of hours should be forbidden, yet the appetite should not, for reasons previously stated, be suffered to grow stale for want of sufficient liquid at meal times in proportion to the solids consumed.

Such views would have been reckoned scandalously heretical twenty-five or more years ago, but the writer feels that he is unorthodox in good company, and is glad to find Mr. E. D. Brickwood, in his treatise on 'Boat-racing,' 1875, laying down his own experiences on the same subject to just the same effect. Mr. Brickwood's remarks on the subject of 'thirst' (as per his index) may be studied with advantage by modern trainers. He says (page 201) :—

As hunger is the warning voice of nature telling us that our bodies are in need of a fresh supply of food, so thirst is the same voice warning us that a fresh supply of liquid is required. Thirst, then, being, like hunger, a natural demand, may safely be gratified, and with water in preference to any other fluid. The prohibition often put upon the use of water or fluid in training may often be carried too far. To limit a man to a pint or two of liquid per day, when his system is throwing off three or four times that quantity through the medium of the ordinary secretions, is as unreasonable as to keep him on half-rations. The general thirst experienced by the whole system, consequent upon great bodily exertion or extreme external heat, has but one means of cure—drink, in the simplest form attainable. Local thirst, usually limited to the mucous linings of the mouth and throat, may be allayed by rinsing the mouth and gargling the throat, sucking the stone of stone fruit, or a pebble, by which to excite the glands in the affected part, or even by dipping the hands into cold water. Fruit is here of very little benefit, as the fluid passes at once to the stomach, and affords no relief to the parts affected; but after rinsing the mouth, small quantities may be swallowed slowly. The field for the selection of food to meet the waste of the body under any condition of physical exertions is by no means restricted. All that the exceptional requirements of training call for is to make a judicious selection; but, in recognising this principle, rowing men have formed a dietary composed almost wholly of restrictions the effect of which has been to produce a sameness in diet which has almost been as injurious in some cases as the entire absence of any laws would be in others.

It should be borne in mind that Mr. Brickwood's field as an amateur lay principally in sculling, which entailed solitary training, unlike that of a member of an eight or four. He had therefore to train himself, and to trust to his own judgment when so doing, blending self-denial with discretion. He is, in the above quotation, apparently speaking of the principles under which he governed himself when training. That they were crowned with good success his record as an athlete shows, for he twice won the Diamond Sculls, and also held the Wingfield (amateur championship) in 1861. Such testimony therefore is the more valuable coming from a successful and self-trained sculler.

As regards sleep, the writer lays great stress upon obtaining a good amount of it. Even if a night is sultry, and sleep does not come easily, still the oarsman can gain something by mere physical repose, though his brain may now and then not obtain rest so speedily as he could wish. The adage ascribed to King George III. as to hours of sleep, 'six for a man, seven for a woman, and eight for a fool,' is unsound. He who is credited with having propounded it, showed in his later years that, either his brain had suffered from deficiency of rest, or that it never had been sufficiently brilliant to justify much attention being bestowed on his philosophy. Probably he never did a really hard day's (still less a week's) labour, of either brain or body, in his life. Had he done so, he would have found that not six, nor seven, and often not eight hours, are too much to enable

M 2

the wasted tissues of brain or body, or both, to recuperate. It is when in a state of repose that the blood, newly made from the latest meal, courses through the system and replenishes what has been wasted during the day. Recruits are never measured for the standard at the end of a day's march, but next day—after a good rest. Cartilage, sinew, muscle, alike waste. The writer used, after racing the Henley course, perhaps thrice in an evening's practice (twice in a four or eight and afterwards in a pair-oar or sculling boat, &c.), to take a good nine hours' sound sleep, and awoke all the better for it. Some men keep on growing to a comparatively late age in life ; such men require more sleep, while thus increasing in size, than others who have earlier attained full bulk and maturity. As a rule, and regardless of what many other trainers may say to the contrary, the writer believes that the majority of men in training may sleep nine hours with advantage.

The period of training varies according to circumstances. A man of twenty-five and upwards, who has been lying by for months, it may be for a year or two, can do with three months of it. The first half should be less severe than the last. He can begin with steady work, to redevelope his muscles, and to reduce his bulk (if he is much over weight) by degrees. The last six weeks should be 'strict' in every sense. He can get into 'hunting' condition in the first six weeks, and progress to 'racing' condition in the succeeding six.

University crews train from five to six weeks. The men are young, and have, most of them, been in good exercise some time before strict training begins.

College crews cannot give much more than three weeks to train for the summer bumping races ; tideway crews have been doing a certain amount of work for weeks before they go into strict training for Henley ; this last stage usually lasts about four weeks.

It is often supposed that a man needs less training for a short than for a long course. This is a mistake. The longer he prepares himself, so long as he does not overdo himself, the better he will be. Long and gradual training is better than short and severe reductions. Over a long course, when an untrained man once finds nature fail him, more ground will be lost than over a short course : *cela va sans dire* : but that is no argument against being thoroughly fit for even a half-mile row. The shorter the course, the higher the pressure of pace, and the crew that cracks first for want of condition—loses (*ceteris paribus*).

Athletes of the running path will agree that it is as impor-

SMOKING IS FORBIDDEN.

tant to train a man thoroughly for a quarter-mile race as for a three-mile struggle. Pace kills, and it is condition which enables the athlete to endure the pace.

Smoking is, as every schoolboy knows, forbidden in training. However, *pro formâ*, the fact must be recorded that it is illicit. It spoils the freedom of the lungs, which should be as elastic as possible, in order to enable them to oxygenate properly the extra amount of blood which circulates under violent exertions.

Aperients at the commencement of training used to be *de*

rigueur. Young men of active habits hardly need them. Anyhow, no trainer should attempt to administer them on his own account ; if he thinks the men need physic at the outset, let him call in a medical man to prescribe for them.

WORK.

We have said that proper diet keeps an oarsman up to the work which is necessary to bring him into good condition. Having detailed the *régime* of diet, and its appurtenances, such as sleep, we may now deal with the system of work itself.

One item of work we have incidentally dealt with, to wit, the morning walk ; but it was necessary to handle this detail at that stage because it had a reference to the morning tub and morning meal.

The work which is set for a crew should be guided by the distance of time from the race. If possible, oarsmen should have their work lightened somewhat towards the close of training, and it is best to get over the heavy work, which is designed to reduce weight as well as to clear the wind, at a comparatively early stage of the training.

There is also another factor to be taken into calculation by the trainer, and that is whether, at the time when sharp work is necessary to produce condition, his crew are sufficiently advanced as oarsmen to justify him in setting them to perform that work at a fast stroke in the boat. Not all crews require to be worked upon the same system, irrespective of the question of stamina and health.

Suppose a crew are backward as oarsmen and also behindhand in condition. If such a crew are set to row a fast stroke in order to blow themselves and to accustom their vascular system to high pressure, their style may be damaged. If on the other hand they do no work except rowing at a slow stroke until within a few days of the race, they will come to the post short of condition. Such a crew should be kept at a slow stroke in the boat, in order to enable them to learn style, for a fortnight or so ; but meantime the trainer should put them through some sharp work upon their legs. He should set them to run a mile or so after the day's rowing. This will get off flesh, and will clear the wind, and meantime style can be studied in the boat. Long rows without an easy are a mistake for backward men who are also short of work. When the pupil gets blown at the end of a few minutes he relapses into his old faults, and makes his last state worse than the first.

Training not only gets

'RUN A MILE OR TWO.'

off superfluous flesh, but also lays on muscle. The sooner the fat is off the sooner does the muscle lay on. The commissariat feeds the newly developing muscles better if there is no tax upon it to replenish the fat as well. For this reason, apart from the importance of clearing the wind, heavy work should come early in training. When a crew who have been considerably reduced in weight early in their course of training, feed up towards the last, and gain in weight, it is a good sign, and shows that their labours have been judiciously adjusted ; the weight which they pick up at the close of training is new muscle replacing the discarded fat.

In training college eights for summer races there is not scope for training on the above system. The time is too short, some of the men are already half-fit, and have been in work of some sort or other during the spring ; while one or two of them may have been lying idle for a twelvemonth. In such cases a captain must use his own discretion ; he can set his grosser men to do some running while he confines those who are fitter to work only in the ship. As a rule, however, unless men have no surplus flesh to take off, all oarsmen are the better for a little running at the end of the day during the early part of training. It prepares their wind for the time when a quick stroke will be required of them. A crew who have been rowing a slow stroke and who have meantime been improved in condition by running, will take to the quick stroke later on more kindly than a ditto class crew who have done no running, and whose condition has been obtained only by rowing exercise. The latter crew have been rowing all abroad while short of wind, and have thereby not corrected, and probably have contracted, faults. The former crew will have had better opportunities of improving their style, will be more like machinery, and will be less blown when they are at last asked to gallop in the boat.

For the first few days it will be well to row an untrained crew over easy half-miles. A long day's work in the boat will not harm them : on the contrary, it will tend to shake them together ; tired men can row well as to style, but men out of breath cannot row. At the end of a week or so, the men can cover a mile at a hard slow grind without an easy. If there is plenty of time, i.e. some five weeks of training, a good deal of paddling can be done, alternating with hard rowing at a slow stroke. If there are only three weeks to train, and men are gross, much paddling cannot be spared. If again time is short and men have already been in work for other races, and do not want much if any reduction in weight, then a good deal of the day's work may be done at a paddle.

Thirty strokes a minute is plenty for slow rowing. Some strokes, though good to race behind, have a difficulty in rowing slow; especially after having had a spell at a fast stroke. It is important to inculcate upon the stroke that thirty a minute should be his 'walking' pace, and should always be maintained except when he is set to do a course, or a part of one, or to row a start. When once he is told to do something like racing over a distance, he must calculate his stroke to orders, whether thirty-two, -four, -six, -eight, &c. But when the 'gallop' is over, then the normal 'thirty' should resume. It is during the 'off' work, when rowing or paddling to or from a course, that there is most scope for coaching, and faults are best cured at a slow stroke.

In training for a short course, such as Henley and college races, a crew may be taken twice each day backwards and forwards over the distance ; the first time at thirty a minute each way, the second time at the 'set' pace of the day, over the course, relapsing into the usual 'thirty' on the reverse journey. The 'set' stroke depends on the stage of training. A fortnight before the race the crew may begin to cover the course, on the second journey, at about thirty-one a minute. A stroke a day can be added to this, until racing pace is reached. If men seem stale, an off-day should be given at light work. Meantime, each day, attention should be paid to 'starting,' so that all may learn to get hold of the first stroke well together. In order to accustom the men to a quicker stroke and to getting forward faster, a few strokes may be rowed, in each start, at a pace somewhat in advance of the rate of stroke set for the day's grind over the course. A couple such starts as this per diem benefit both crew and coach. The crew begin to feel what a faster stroke will be like, without being called upon to perform it over the whole distance before they are fit to go ; the coach will be able to observe each man's work at the faster stroke. Many a green oarsman looks promising while the stroke is slow, but becomes all abroad when called upon to row fast. It is best to have some insight to these possible failings early in training, else it may be too late to remedy them or to change the man on the eve of battle.

Towards the close of training the crew should do their level best once or twice over the course, to accustom them to being rowed out, and to give them confidence in their recuperative powers ; also to enable the stroke to feel the power of his crew, and to form an opinion as to how much he can ask them to do in the race. The day before the racing begins, work should be light.

In bumping races, if a college has no immediate fear of foes from the rear, it is well not to bring men too fine to the post ; else, though they may do well enough for the first day or two, they may work stale or lose power before the end of the six days of the contest. It is better that a crew should row itself into condition than out of it. In training for long-distance racing, it is customary to make about every alternate day a light one, of about the same work as for college racing. The other days are long-course days of long grinds, to get men together, and to reduce weight. When men have settled to a light boat, and have begun to row courses against time, and especially when they reach Putney water, two long courses in each week are about enough. Many crews do not do even so much as this. As a rule a crew are better for not being taken for more than ten or eleven minutes of hard, uninterrupted racing, within three days of the race. A long course wastes much tissue, and it takes a day or two to feed up what they have wasted. Nevertheless, crews have been known to do long courses within 48 hours of a Putney match, and to win withal : e.g. the Oxonians of 1883, who came racing pace from Barnes to Putney two days before the race, and 'beat record' over that stretch of water.

Strokes and coaches do a crew much harm if they are jealous of 'times' prematurely in practice. Suppose an opponent does a fast time, there is no need to go to the starting point and endeavour to eclipse time. Possibly his rapid time has been accomplished by dint of a prematurely rapid stroke, while the pace of our own boat, with regard to the rate of stroke employed, discloses promise of better pace than our opponents, when racing shall arrive in real earnest. Now if we, for jealousy, take our own men at a gallop before they are ripe for it, we run great risk of injuring their style, and of throwing them back instead of improving them. After the day's race, the body should be well washed in tepid water, and rubbed dry with rough towels. It is a good thing for an oarsman to keep a toothbrush in his dressing-room. He will find it a great relief against thirst to wash his mouth out with it when dressing, more especially so if he also uses a little tincture of myrrh.

One 'odd man' is of great service to training, even if he cannot spare time to row in the actual race. Many a man in a crew is the better for a day's, or half a day's, rest now and then. Yet his gain is loss of practice to the rest, unless a stop-gap can be found to keep the machinery going. The berth of ninth man in a University eight often leads to promotion to the full colours in a following season, as U.B.C. records can show.

With college eights there used to be a *furore*, some twenty years ago, for taking them over the long course in a gig eight. These martyrs, half fit, were made to row the regulation long course, from 'first gate' to lasher, or at least to Nuneham railway bridge, at a hard and without an easy. The idea was to 'shake them together.' The latter desideratum could have been attained just as well by taking them to the lasher and back again, but allowing them to be eased once in each mile or so. Many crews that adopted the process met with undoubted success, but we fancy that their success would have been greater had their long row been judiciously broken by rest every five minutes. To behold a half-trained college eight labouring past Nuneham, at the end of some fifteen minutes of toil, jealous to beat the time of some rival crew, used to be a pitiable sight. More crews were marred than made by this fanaticism.

On the morning of a race it is a good thing to send a crew to run sprints of seventy or eighty yards, twice. This clears the wind greatly for the rest of the day, without taking any appreciable strength out of the man. A crew thus 'aired' do not so much feel the severity of a sharp start in the subsequent race, and they gain their second wind much sooner.

The meal before a race should be a light one, comparatively: something that can be digested very easily. Mutton is digested sooner than beef. H. Kelley used to swear by a wing of boiled chicken (without sauce) before a race. The fluid should be kept as low as possible just before a race ; and there should be about three hours between the last meal and the start. A preliminary canter in the boat is advisable ; it tests all oars and stretchers, and warms up the muscles. Even when men are rowing a second or third race in the day, they should not be chary of extending themselves for a few strokes on the way to the post. Muscles stiffen after a second race, and are all the better for being warmed up a trifle before they are again placed on the rack.

Between races a little food may be taken, even if there is only an hour to spare : biscuit soaked in port wine stays the stomach ; and if there is more than an hour cold mutton and stale bread (no butter), to the extent of a couple of sandwiches or more (according to time for digestion), will be of service. Such a meal may be washed down with a little cold tea and brandy. The tea deadens the pain of stiffened muscles ; the brandy helps to keep the pulse up. If young hands are fidgetty and nervous, a little brandy and water may be given them ; or brandy and tea, not exceeding a wine-glass, rather more tea than brandy. The writer used often to pick up his crew thus, and was sometimes laughed at for it in old days. He is relieved to find no less an authority than Mr. E. D. Brickwood, on page 219 of 'Boat-racing,' holding the same view as himself, and commending the same system of 'pick-me-up.'

AILMENTS.

A rowing man seems somehow to be heir to nearly as many ailments as a racehorse. Except that he does not turn 'roarer,' and that there is no such hereditary taint in rowing clubs, he may almost be likened to a Derby favourite.

Boils are one of the most common afflictions. They used to be seen more frequently in the writer's days than now. The modern recognition of the importance of a due proportion of vegetable food blended with the animal food has tended to reduce the proportion of oarsmen annually laid up by this complaint. A man is not carnivorous purely, but omnivorous, like a pig or a bear. If he gorges too much animal food meat, he disorders his blood, and his blood seeks to throw off its humours. If there is a sore anywhere on the frame at the time, the blood will select this as a safety valve, and will raise a fester there. If there is no such existing safety valve, the blood soon broaches a volcano of its own, and has an unpleasant habit of selecting most inconvenient sites for these eruptions. Where there is most wear and tear going on to the cuticle is a likely spot for the volcano to open, and nature in this respect is prone to favour the seat of honour more than any other portions of the frame. Next in fashion, perhaps, comes the neck ; the friction of a comforter when the neck is dripping with perspiration tends often to make the skin of the neck tender and to induce a boil to break out there. A blistered hand is not unlikely to be selected as the scene of outbreak, or a shoulder chafed by a wet jersey.

A crew should be under strict orders to report *all* ailments, if only a blister, *instantly* to the coach. It is better to leave *no* discretion in this matter to the oarsman, even at the risk of troubling the mentor with trifles. If a man is once allowed to decide for himself whether he will report some petty and incipient ailment, he is likely to try to hush it up lest it should militate against his coach's selection of him ; the effect of this is that mischief which might otherwise have been checked in the bud, is allowed to assume dangerous proportions for want of a stitch in time. An oarsman should be impressed that nothing is more likely to militate against his dream of being selected than disobedience to this or any other standing order. The smallest pimple should be shown forthwith to the coach, the slightest hoarseness or tendency to snuffle reported ; any tenderness of joint or sinew instantly made known.

To return to boils. If a boil is observed in the pimple stage, it may be scotched and killed. Painting it with iodine will drive it away, in the writer's experience. 'Stonehenge', advises a wash of nitrate of silver, of fifteen to twenty grains to the ounce, to be painted over the spot. Mr. Brickwood also, while quoting 'Stonehenge' on this point, recommends bathing with bay salt and water.

Anyhow, these external means of repression do not of themselves suffice. They only bung up the volcano ; the best step is to cure the blood, otherwise it will break out somewhere else. The writer's favourite remedy is a dose of syrup of iodide of iron; one teaspoonful in a wineglass of water, just before or after a meal, is about the best thing. A second dose of half the amount may be taken twenty-four hours later. This medicine is rather constipating ; a slight aperient, if only a dose of Carlsbad salts before breakfast or a seidlitz powder, may be taken to counteract it in this respect. It is a strong but prompt remedy ; anything is better than to have a member of a crew eventually unable to sit down for a week or so ! An extra glass of port after dinner, *and plenty of green food*, will help to rectify the disordered blood.

Another good internal remedy is brewer's yeast, a tablespoonful twice a day after meals. Watermen swear by this, and Mr. Brickwood personally recommends it.

If care is taken a boil can be thus nipped in the bud (figuratively) ; to do this *literally* is the very worst thing. Some people pinch off the head of a small boil. This only adds fuel to the fire. If a boil has become large, red, and angry before any remedies are applied, it is too late to drive it in, and the next best thing is to coax it out. This is done with strong linseed poultices. A doctor should be called in, and be persuaded to lance it, to the core, and to squeeze it, so soon as he judges it to be well filled with pus.

Raws used to be more common twenty-five years ago than

now : boat cushions had much to do with them. Few oarsmen in these days use cushions. Raws are best anointed with a mixture of oxide of zinc, spermaceti and glycerine, which any chemist can make up, to the consistency of cold cream. It should be buttered on thickly, especially at bed-time.

Blisters should be pricked with a needle (*never* with a *pin*); the water should be squeezed out, and the old skin left on to shield the young skin below.

Festers are only another version of boils. The internal remedies, to rectify the blood, should be the same as for boils. Cuts or wounds of broken skin may be treated like raws if slight ; if deeper, then wrapped in lint, soaked in cold water, and bound with oilskin to keep the lint moist.

Abdominal strains sometimes occur (i.e. of the abdominal muscles of recovery) if a man does a hard day's work before he is fairly fit. A day's rest is the best thing ; an hour's sitting in a hot hip bath, replenishing the heat as the water cools, gives much relief. The strain works off while the oarsman is warm to his work, but recurs with extra pain when he starts cold for the next row. If there is any suspicion of hernia (or ' rupture ') work should instantly stop, even ten miles from home ; the patient should row no more, walk gently to a resting-place, and send for a doctor. Once only has the writer known of real hernia in a day's row, and then the results were painfully serious. Inspection of the abdomen will show if there is any hernia.

Diarrhœa is a common complaint. It is best to call in a doctor if the attack does not pass off in half a day. If a man has to go to the post while thus affected, it is a good thing to give him some *raw* arrowroot (three or four table-spoonfuls) in *cold* water. The dose should be well stirred, to make the arrowroot swill down the throat. To put the arrowroot into hot water spoils the effect which is desired.

Many doctors have a tender horror of consenting to any patient rowing, even for a day, so long as he is under their care, though only for a boil which does not affect his action.

Professional instinct prompts them to feel that the speediest possible cure is the chief desideratum, and of course that object is best attained by lying on the shelf. A doctor who will consent to do his best to cure, subject to assenting to his patient's continuing at work so long as actual danger is not thereby incurred, and so long as disablement for the more important race day is not risked, is sometimes, but too rarely, found.

Sprains, colds, coughs, &c., had better be submitted at once to a doctor. A cold on the chest may become much more serious than it appears at first, and should never be trifled with. Slightly sprained wrists weaken, but need not necessarily cripple a man. Mr. W. Hoare, stroke of Oxford boat in 1862, had a sprained wrist at Putney, and rowed half the race with only one hand, as also much of the practice. He was none the worse after Easter, when the tendons had rested and recuperated.

Oarsmen should be careful to wrap up warmly the instant that they cease work. Many a cold has been caught by men sitting in their jerseys—cold wind suddenly checking perspiration after a sharp row—while some chatter is going on about the time which the trial has taken, or why No. So-and-so caught a small crab halfway. A woollen comforter should always be at hand to wrap promptly round the neck and over the chest when exertion ceases, and so soon as men land they should clothe up in warm flannel, until the time comes to strip and work.

Siestas should not be allowed. There is a temptation to doze on a full stomach after a hard day, or even when fresh after a midday meal. No one should be allowed to give way to this ; it only makes men ' slack,' and spoils digestion.

If a man can keep his bedclothes on all night, and keep warm, he will do himself good if he sleeps with an open window, winter or summer. He thereby gets more fresh air, and accordingly has not to tax the respiratory muscles so much, in order to inhale the necessary amount of oxygen. Eight hours' sleep with open windows refresh the frame more than nine hours and upwards in a stuffy bedroom. A roaring fire may obviate an open window, for it forces a constant current of air through the apartment. The writer has slept with windows wide open, winter and summer, since he first matriculated at his University, save once or twice for a night or two when suffering from cold (not contracted by having slept with open windows). If a bed is well tucked up, and the frame well covered, the chest cannot be chilled, and the mouth and nose are none the worse for inhaling cool fresh air, even below freezing-point. This refers to men of sound chests. Men of weak constitution have no business to train or to race.

HANDLING BOATS UNDER OARS

A boat is defined by Webster as "a small open vessel, or watercraft, usually moved by oars or rowing."

A deepwater man considers a boat any small craft, usually auxiliary to his own larger ship, which can be bodily lifted from the water and stowed on a large vessel.

With the coming of power and modern sail rigs, replacing oars, the "boat" has reached far beyond its meaning of only a few decades ago. For the purposes of this manual, a boat shall be considered any hull however moved which is not a ship. This, of course, raises the question: how small is a ship; as well as other questions even more embarrassing. So, rather than place a limit of size or tonnage to the vessels to which this manual applies, let us merely state that the canoeist, the small-sailboat man, the powerboat man should find this work advanced and complete while the deepwater merchant or naval sailor should find it elemental and complete, lacking only full treatment of specialized subjects.

In most cases the boat is operated singlehanded; the lone operator must be his own deck man, navigator, reefer, engineer, and cook; serve his vessel as owner, master, and crew. He must thoroughly understand the elements of a great many subjects—be his vessel a dinghy, a 40-ton schooner, or a dragger—and he must have a basic working knowledge of them all.

Before he ever steps foot on his boat, certainly before he will require a knowledge of detailed seamanship, navigation, or maintenance, he will need to understand the handling of the boat of his choice.

Logically, a manual purporting to be complete and useful should commence at the beginning—at boat handling.

Logically, the subject of boat handling should commence at the beginning also—with the handling of the basic elemental type of boat, that which is propelled by man power.

HANDLING BOATS UNDER OARS

The ancient, straddling his logboat, without doubt first propelled his rude craft by a setting pole, a satisfactory device until he sailed into deep water. Once "off soundings" he was up against trouble, and his answer was to kick his feet violently and discover that the broad bulk of his calves actually moved his boat independently of any contact with the solid land beneath him. It was a short step from this discovery to the conversion of his spare setting pole to a paddle by attaching a wide, flat section of bark to it. The need for an efficient means of propelling larger craft led to a further evolution of the paddle to an oar.

The types of rowing boats are myriad. Each region has developed its own peculiar type best suited to wind, weather, and beaching conditions as well as to basic purposes. In general the dory is considered the safest deepwater boat. It is high-sided and has marked *flare,* making it a good weight carrier and a fairly dry boat. Its construction is strong enough not to depend upon thwarts for strength, and so it can be nested or banked, four or more dories to a bank. It is generally rowed by pushing the oars rather than pulling them, the boatman facing forward in a standing position. Dories will sail only moderately well, and they require a small sail with low centers.

In very small sizes the flat-bottomed rowboat is satisfactory and is easily pulled except in very rough water. It is a good carrier and is strong, but it can seldom be towed satisfactorily. However, it has the advantages of cheapness, ease in building and repair, and of being able to take a lot of punishment on a beach or at a wharf; and is a common type. Properly designed and taken out of the "box" class, the flat-bottomed, or sharpie, rowboat makes the best all-round boat for most small-boat uses.

Round and V-bottomed small boats are treacherous, cranky craft until they reach a length of about 12 feet. In the smaller sizes they have most of the bad characteristics of the canoe and none of its good characteristics. They tow fairly well, they can be sailed, and they look well in conjunction with a smart yacht when davited or decked. Repairs are difficult. Unless very lightly built, they are heavier than the flat-bottomed boat and therefore offer more difficulty in beaching and stowing. In larger sizes, such as cutters and whaleboats, the advantages of round-bottomed construction and design become apparent, and they become able boats.

In selecting the small boat the prime consideration should be that it fit the uses to which it will be put.

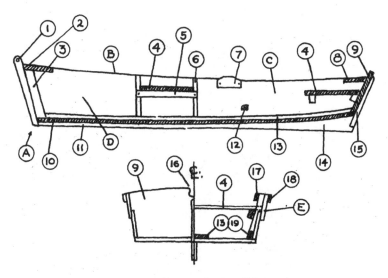

Figure 101. Parts of a Small Boat

1. False stem	10. Bottom plank
2. Breasthook	11. Keel
3. Stempost	12. Stretcher
4. Thwart (seat)	13. Keelson
5. Riser	14. Skag
6. Rib (or frame)	15. Sternpost
7. Socket block	16. Sculling notch
8. Quarter knee	17. Gunwale (or clamp)
9. Transom	18. Rub mold (or gunwale)

19. Clintle (nailing strip)

A. Forefoot   C. Stern sheets
B. Sheer (curvature)   D. Foresheets
E. Sheer strake

101. The Flat-bottomed rowboat up to 12 feet. For lake and river recreation and fishing, protected salt-water fishing, dinghy use, work boats; outboard motors up to about four hp. Sail well except to windward in a rough water.

102. The Dory up to 21 feet. For exposed waters and offshore. Tenders for deepwater boats. Unless sections are modified (*see* Figure 102) will not sail well except off the wind.

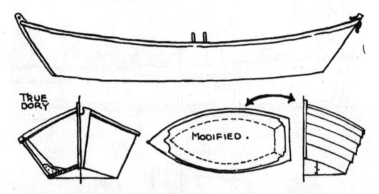

Figure 102. The Dory. Right, Modified for Sailing or Outboard Motor

103. The Round-bottomed boat (and V-bottomed). Good, "fancy" dinghies in small sizes. Drive well under power and tow well. When so designed will sail very well. (Example: the "Frost-bite" dinghies.) Boats carried by ships are always round-bottomed and reach the length of 40 feet.

THE OAR

104. Ash makes the best oar material. It may be kept white and clean by rubbing with sand and canvas. Always stow oars flat. For long life, the leather (which may be of leather, canvas, or fiber) is necessary. (Figure 104.)

Rules for length:

In a single-banked boat (whaler)—twice the width of the thwart from which it is rowed plus the freeboard at the rowlock.

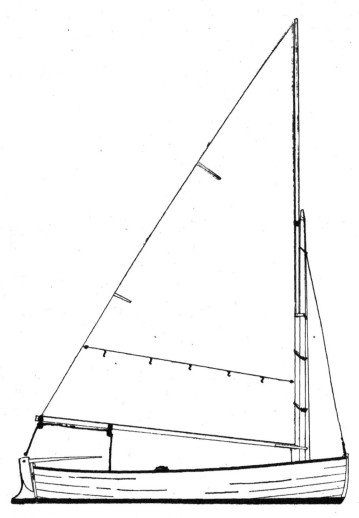

Figure 103. 13-Foot Utility Round Bottom Dinghy for Sail, Power, or Rowing

In a double-banked boat (cutter)—twice the length of the thwart from which it is rowed.

In a single-hander (dinghy)— 7' OA 6' oar
9' OA 6½' oar
11' OA 7' oar
13' OA 7½' oar

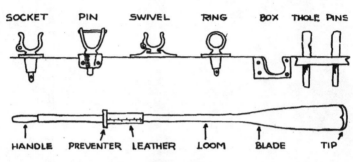

SOCKET   PIN   SWIVEL   RING   BOX   THOLE PINS

HANDLE   PREVENTER LEATHER   LOOM   BLADE   TIP

Figure 104.

Rowing the Small Boat

105. Most good oarsmen prefer to have the ends of the oar handles touch each other or even overlap slightly. Either way, the result will be considerably more power than when the handles are widely separated.

The complete stroke is made up of four distinct parts:
Catch—Place the blade in the water, ready to pull.
Pull—Sweep the blade aft to give headway.
Feather—Raise the blade out of the water and turn flat.
Recover—Swing oars to position of *Catch*.
To give the stroke power it is essential to:
1. Keep the upper edge of the blade at the surface of the water.
2. Keep hands about level. They move fore and aft as if in a fixed groove.
3. As the stroke is completed, the wrist is given a smart flip so that the blade comes out of the water at about a 45° angle. The elbows are in close to the body.
4. Keep the back straight, chin up and in, and the feet against the stretcher.
   Your weight should be centered slightly abaft the center of buoyancy; never so that the boat trims down by the head.

The pin-type lock (Figure 104) will not permit proper rowing form. It is popular on lakes for trolling where the oars must be trailed at times. Better is a ring rowlock and a preventer inboard of the oar leather.

Learn to set a course and head the boat exactly for it (making due allowances for tide or wind if necessary). From then on steer by the

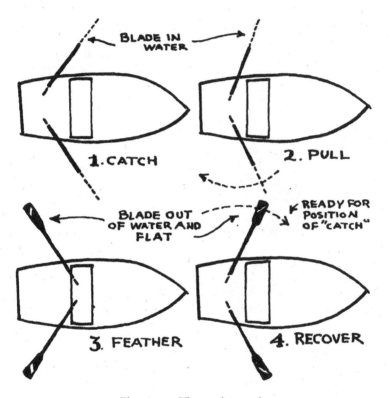

Figure 105. The rowing stroke

wake or by taking ranges over some point of the quarter. It is lubberly and tiresome to peer forward after every few strokes.

Long pulls can be made less tedious by changing the position of the oars slightly or by facing forward and push-rowing for a while. More progress will be made against a head sea by quartering into it rather than meeting the seas head on. This is especially true with a flat-bottomed boat of generous beam.

Sculling

106. A single oar, properly handled, can move a boat almost as fast as a pair of oars used in the usual manner. This maneuver is called sculling, and it is especially useful in congested waters, such as near a busy dock or in a narrow creek or channel.

The oar is shipped over the stern, or the quarter, in a rowlock or through a grommet that has been spliced into the transom, the

Figure 106. **Sculling**: Right, the Successive Blade Positions

sculler standing and facing aft. The oar is placed with the blade athwart the boat. Grasp the handle in the right hand, turn the knuckles down, and move the handle to the right. At the end of the stroke, turn the knuckles up and move the handle to the left—knuckles up, push left; knuckles down, push right. Continue, and keep the oar blade pressing outboard—that's all there is to sculling. Steering is accomplished by easing the motion right or left, and so directing the boat.

Boat Orders

107. Boat orders are given by the coxswain. Their practical use is in training for rowing in unison with a pulling boat's crew, such as that of a life boat or a surf boat. "Oars" is a hold position midway between the stroke parts of "feather" and "recover." "Stand by" is the commencement of "pull" but the oars are not yet dipped awaiting the command "Give way." It is smart to flip the oars from "pull" to "recover" with a slight upward turn of the blade.

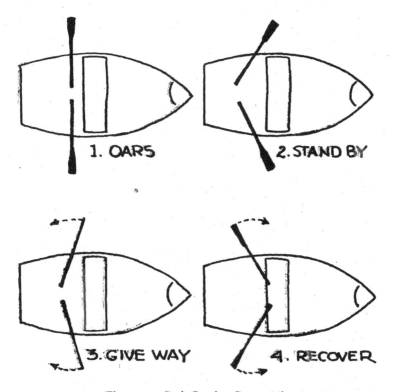

Figure 107. Basic Rowing Commands

Handling Ship's Boats Under Oars

108. Boats manning four or more oars use a set form of commands in handling. These are given by the coxswain (steersman) and are used according to the following tables:

TABLE I

Used by cutters with sunken or box rowlocks.

(1) *Stand by the oars.*
(2) *Up oars.*
    (1 and 2 *given before the boat is reported ready.*)
(3) *Shove off.*
(4) *Let fall.*
(5) *Give way together.*
(6) *In bows.*
(7) *Stand by to toss, Toss,* or *Oars* (followed by *Boat the oars* or *Way enough,* without the command *Oars*).

In all other cases the commands in Table II shall be used to shove off and go alongside. Boats with swivel rowlocks will not toss oars, and boats with awnings spread cannot toss oars.

TABLE II

(1) *Stand by the oars.*
(2) *Shove off.*
(3) *Out oars.*
(4) *Give way together.*
(5) *In bows,* or *Trail bow.*
(6) *Oars* (followed by *Boat the oars* or *Way enough,* without the command *Oars*).

THE SPECIAL COMMANDS FOLLOWING ARE FOR USE IN THE SITUATIONS INDICATED.

Out oars.—To rig out the oars in the rowlocks ready for pulling.

Oars.—(1) To salute. (2) To stop pulling for any purpose, keeping the oars out, horizontal and blades feathered.

Give way together (starboard, port).—To commence pulling.

Trail.—(1) To salute. (2) To pass obstructions. For the latter, oars of either side may be trailed independently.

Hold water.—To check headway or sternway. The oars of either side may hold water independently. If boat has much headway, care is required.

Stern all.—To acquire sternway. Should not be given when boat has much headway. When boat has headway, should be preceded by *Hold water.*

EXPLANATION OF THE COMMANDS:

Figure 108A .

Stand by the oars.—Every man except the bowman seizes his oar by its handle and sees the blade clear of other oars. The oars should be shoved forward over the gunwale far enough to bring the handle in the proper position, but should be kept fore and aft. The blades will be kept clear of the bowmen's boat hooks.

Figure 108B

Out oars.—Given when the boat is clear of the ship's side. Thwartmen throw blades of oars horizontally outward, allowing the leathers to fall in rowlocks, place both hands on handle, and quickly trim blades flat and directly abeam. This is the position of *Oars.* Bowmen throw their oars at the same time as rest of crew, if they are ready; otherwise, they swing their oars out together, touching their blades forward to insure making the movements in unison, and bring them to the position of *Oars* to take up the stroke with the remainder of the crew, as the case may be.

Figure 108C

Trail.—Given when blades are in the water. Finish that stroke, release the handle of the oar, allowing it to draw fore and aft and trail alongside. If no trailing lines are fitted, retain the handle of the oar in the hand. With a cutter having sunken rowlocks, lift the handle of the oar quickly when blade is in the water at middle of stroke, throw oar out of rowlock, and retain handle in hand.

Figure 108D

Point the oars.—To shove off a boat that has grounded, stand facing aft, point the blades of the oars forward and downward to the beach at an angle of about 30°, ready to shove off at the command. If waves lift the stern of the boat, the united effort to shove off should be made just as her stern lifts.

Figure 108E

Give way together.—All the oarsmen take the full stroke, keeping accurate stroke with the starboard stroke oar. Feather blades habitually. Bowmen get out their oars together and take up the stroke. (They may have got them out before the command *Give way together,* in which case they give way with the other members of the crew.)

Handling Boats Under Oars

Figure 108F

Way enough.—If the crew has the skill, the command *Way enough* makes a fancy and snappy landing at a dock or gangway. Ordinarily, the command *Oars* is given, whereupon the stroke is completed and the oars brought to the position of *Out oars.* (Figure 108B.) *In bows* is given as the boat drifts to its objective, the bowmen boating their oars and, manning the boat hooks, springing to position in the fore-sheets, ready to fend or hold on. The command *Boat the oars* (the reverse of *Stand by oars*) will permit the landing to be made.

Back starboard (port).—To turn. Should *Hold water* before backing, if boat has much headway.

Back starboard, Give way port (or vice versa).—To turn quickly when boat has little or no headway.

Stand by to toss, Toss.—Used only in cutter, with sunken rowlocks. (1) To salute. (2) In going alongside, when it is not desirable to boat the oars. The habitual command to be used when coming alongside. Given from position of *Oars.*

Boat the oars.—To get the oars into the boat. Given when lying on oars, or when oars have been tossed or trailed.

Point the oars.—To shove off a grounded or beached boat.

Way enough.—To cease pulling and boat the oars. Given only while pulling, and for proper execution must be given just as the blades enter the water.

Let fall.—To go from *Up oars* to *Oars.*

(*Note.*—Thwarts and oars are numbered from forward. Double-banked thwarts are designated by No. 1, starboard, No. 1, port; No. 2, starboard, No. 2, port, etc. The thwarts next to the bow and stroke are also properly designated as second bow and second stroke.)

UNITED STATES COAST GUARD ROWING INSTRUCTIONS

Pulling by Numbers

109. The crew is first taught to pull by numbers as follows: From the position of *Oars* the order is given to *Stand by*. At this order the body is bent forward at the hips and between the thighs, back straight, shoulders braced back, the arms extended to the full extent, the knees well apart, chest and belly full and prominent. The blade of the oar should be at right angles to the water and about one foot above it. Both hands should grasp the oar handle with the thumbs underneath. The head must be kept erect, the eyes on the back of the man in front.

1.—Drop the blades of the oars into the water without chop or splash. As the oar enters the water (keeping the surface of the blade perpendicular), put the weight of the body on the oar, arms and back remaining straight; drive with the legs against the stretcher until they are straightened out and the body is about $22\frac{1}{2}°$ past the perpendicular. The body must then remain stationary, while the arms bring the oar home by bending the elbows and keeping them close to the body until the root of the thumb touches the breast about one inch below the nipple.

NOTE:—The knees during this movement should close slightly. This movement is an excellent exercise for strengthening the muscles of the back, thighs, stomach, and loins, which play such an important part in rowing. The stroke should be begun by trying to feel the water, and it should then develop into a hard, steady pull.

2.—Drop the arms until the blade is clear of the water.

3.—Turn the wrists by dropping them, bringing the knuckles up, and feathering the oar.

4.—Shoot the arms out sharply, but without a jerk, and swing the body slowly and steadily forward to the position of *Stand by*. Care should be taken that the body comes steadily aft, otherwise the oarsmen will drop their shoulders and heads, and the blades, instead of being as close to the water as possible on the return, are uneven and cannot enter the water together.

After the motions have been distinctly taught, combine the first, second, and third at the order *Stroke,* completing the fourth motion at the word *Recover.*

When the crews have been thoroughly practiced in the combination, pulling in quick time should be carried out, the order being to *Give way.*

Cadets should always remember that the main object is to pull correctly, and that pulling hard and for a long distance is merely a matter of practice; but that a bad style once contracted is like a bad habit, hard to get out of. It must be impressed upon the boat's crew that their oars are to be pulled more by their legs than by their arms, and that both hands, both arms, both shoulders, each loin, and both legs and feet should bear an equal strain throughout the stroke.

The stroke should be finished with the shoulders and the muscles that work them, and the biceps should be passive throughout the stroke.

The whole secret of pulling lies in the body swing and good leg work against the stretcher.

LAYING ON OARS:—At the order *Oars* the crew will come to the position *Oars,* as previously described, taking time from the stroke oars.

1. SWING:—The aim in this should be to swing the body as far as possible from the hips without bending the back, being careful to let the head swing with the body. The swing must be slow and balanced, for the time occupied in coming forward should be the body's rest, when the easy, measured swing, erect head, braced shoulders, and open chest enable heart and lungs to work freely and easily, in preparation for a definite beginning of the next stroke. As the body swings, the hands should be at the same time stretching and reaching out, as if striving to touch something which is constantly evading them.

2. STRAIGHT BACKS:—As far as possible, a straight back should be acquired. The values of a straight back are as follows:

(a) The swing must be from the hips, and not from any point in the middle of the back as a secondary pivot.

(b) The straightness of the back eases the respiratory organs.

3. USE OF ARMS:—The arms must be straight when swinging back. They must be considered as merely connecting rods between the body and the oars. The use of the biceps in rowing should be discouraged, as the man who finishes his stroke by the aid of the biceps invariably

sticks his elbows out at right angles to his ribs, thus giving a weak as well as a cramped and ugly finish.

4. DO NOT MEET YOUR OARS:—i. e., keep your body back until your hands have come in. *If you pull yourself forward to meet your oars, you will certainly shorten your stroke prematurely.*

5. TURNING OF HANDS TOWARD END OF STROKE:—Hands must be dropped before the wrists are turned to get the blade clear of the water first, and to insure a neat, clean feather. If the oar is feathered properly it comes out like a knife.

6. USE OF LEGS:—When the beginner has been taught the use of his body and has begun to get used to the swing of it for the main motive power of the stroke, he can be taught to apply extra power with his feet at the right time, to increase the power and the swing of the body. As soon as the body feels the strain of the oar, legs instinctively stiffen themselves against the stretcher. They should be kept in this rigid posture, supporting the body throughout the stroke. The rigidity should commence at the instant the oar touches the water and the strain begins to fall upon the shoulder.

7. RECOVERY:—This is largely dependent upon the abdominal muscles, and to get quick recovery these muscles must be exercised and developed. The muscles of the legs, thighs, and loins should all join with those of the abdomen in the recovery. The first part of the recovery should be the most rapid.

8. CATCH:—The beginning of the stroke should be the most forcible part. This *catch* should be driven from the body as if the whole body were to be lifted off the seat by the joint support of the oar and stretcher. Avoid striking the water in the *catch*.

9. FORM:—May be defined and made up of square shoulders, straight swing from the loins, elastic recovery, and absence of doubling up at the finish.

10. DISTANCE OF SWING BACK:—In deciding this, two things must be considered. Viz.:

(a) Whether the man is physically capable of maintaining his length of *swing back* without sacrificing some of his *reach forward*.

(b) Whether his powers of recovery are adequate to the distance through which his body has to be recovered for the next stroke.

If both of these can be done, then the man who fulfills these conditions is doing his work to best advantage, if his body, when straight at the end of the stroke, makes an angle of about 22½° with the perpendicular, the reach forward being full.

It is more economical to recovery to swing fairly well back and to row a fewer number of long strokes than a large number of short strokes.

In teaching a man to swing back, he should be told to hold his head well up. The weight, if thrown back, assists his swing, while if hanging forward, it acts in a contrary direction.

> *Insist on Silence Being Kept in the Boat.*
> *Insist on Eyes Being Kept in the Boat.*
> *Allow No Inattention.*

Special Notes on Handling Boats under Oars

110. In going into a crowded or difficult landing, pull easily and keep the boat under control with the oars as long as possible, laying on oars if necessary, and boating oars only at the last moment.

In going through a narrow entrance, get good way on the boat, then trail or toss the oars.

A loaded boat holds her way much longer than a light one.

In pulling across a current, try to make good a straight line by steering up stream from the line you want to make good.

Having a long pull against the tide, run near shore where the tide is slacker than in midstream, and where there is sometimes an eddy.

There should always be a lantern, filled and trimmed, in the boat, and boats should never leave for a trip of any great length without a compass. Weather is liable to thicken at any time, and a boat without a compass would have difficulty in reaching a landing or returning to the ship. For this reason, coxswains should at all times know the compass course between the ship and landing; and if they are away from the ship and it begins to thicken, they should at once observe the compass course before the ship is shut in.

Never go alongside a vessel which has sternway or which is backing her engines.

In coming alongside in a seaway or when a strong tide is running, warn the bowman to look out for the boat line which will be heaved from the ship.

If caught in a gale in an open boat, rig a sea anchor by lashing the spars and sails together, sails loosed. Fit a span to this and ride by the painter. If there is oil in the boat, secure a bag full of waste saturated with oil to the sea anchor.

Use of Oil for Modifying the Effect of Breaking Waves

111. Many experiences of late years have shown that the utility of oil for this purpose is undoubted and the application simple. The following may serve for the guidance of seamen whose attention is called to the fact that a very small quantity of oil skillfully applied may prevent much damage, both to ships (especially of the smaller classes) and to the boats, by modifying the action of breaking seas. The principal facts as to the use of oil are as follows:

1. On free waves—that is, waves in deep water—the effect is greatest.

2. In a surf or waves breaking on a bar, where a mass of liquid is in actual motion in shallow water, the effect of the oil is uncertain, as nothing can prevent the larger waves from breaking under such circumstances, but even here it is of some service.

3. The heaviest and thickest oils are most effectual. Refined kerosene is of little use; crude petroleum is serviceable when nothing else is obtainable; but all animal and vegetable oils, and generally waste oil from the engines, have great effect.

4. A small quantity of oil suffices, if applied in such a manner as to spread to windward.

5. It is useful in a ship or boat, either when running or lying to or in wearing.

6. No experiences are related of its use when hoisting a boat at sea or in a seaway, but it is highly probable that much time would be saved and injury to the boat avoided by its use on such occasions.

7. In cold water the oil, being thickened by the lower temperature and not being able to spread freely, will have its effect much reduced. This will vary with the description of oil used.

8. For a ship at sea the best method of application appears to be to hang over the side, in such a manner as to be in the water, small canvas bags capable of holding from one to two gallons of oil, the bags being pricked with a sail needle to facilitate leakage of the oil. The oil is also frequently distributed from canvas bags or oakum inserted in the closet bowls. The positions of these bags should vary with the

circumstances. Running before the wind they should be hung on either bow—for example, from the carhead—and allowed to tow in the water. With the wind on the quarter the effect seems to be less than in any other position, as the oil goes astern while the waves come up on the quarter. Lying to, the weather bow, and another position farther aft seem the best places from which to hang the bags, using sufficient line to permit them to draw to windward while the ship drifts.

9. Crossing a bar with a flood tide, to pour oil overboard and allow it to float in ahead of the boat, which would follow with a bag towing astern, would appear to be the best plan. As before remarked, under these circumstances, the effect cannot be so much trusted. On a bar with the ebb tide running it would seem to be useless to try oil for the purpose of entering.

10. For boarding a wreck it is recommended to pour oil overboard to windward of her before going alongside. The effect in this must greatly depend upon the set of the current and the circumstances of the depth of water.

11. For a boat riding in bad weather from a sea anchor it is recommended to fasten the bag to an endless line rove through a block on the sea anchor, by which means the oil can be diffused well ahead of the boat and the bag readily hauled on board for refilling if necessary.

Towing, Decking, Daviting Small Boats

112. Towing the small boat has ever been a problem of the cruiser, especially in a sea or offshore. Dangers include swamping and filling and consequent strain and perhaps parting of the towing hawser and, under certain conditions, the towed boat actually coming aboard the towing craft or ramming her stern.

Experienced deepwater men insist upon a deck design which allows the small boat to be carried there or in davits.

If the boat must be towed it is best secured to a quarter bitt. Towed off center thus it exerts somewhat less pull and is less apt to "wander" in its course astern. Sometimes this inclination to veer can be cured quite easily by:

1. Dragging a length of line from the *center* of the towed boat.
2. Affixing a deeper or longer skeg.

111

3. Ballasting the towed boat a trifle out of trim, port, starboard, or by the stern.

4. Lashing the tiller (if so equipped) to keep the towed boat edging slightly off the true course.

5. Towing the boat at "just the right" point aft, the point to be found by experimenting, and depending upon speed, sea conditions, tide, and current. In a towing boat having a distinct wave drag this spot is likely to be the forward side of the second following wave.

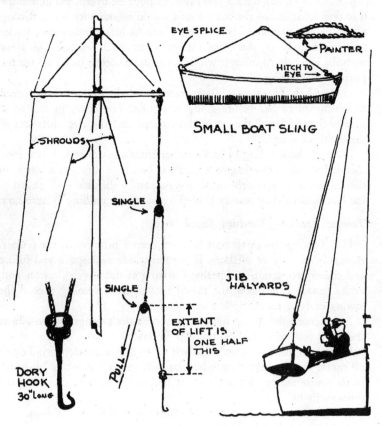

Figure 113. Two Methods of Decking a Small Boat

Handling Boats Under Oars

Most small boats tow best if provided with a towing ring on the stem near the waterline or even below it. This gives a lift to the forefoot which prevents the boat from "nosing" (burying the forefoot) and veering wildly.

113. Some method of actually taking the dinghy aboard the larger boat is necessary for any extended coastwise work. Davits are an abomination on the small cruiser unless there is beam enough to davit the small boat thwartships across the stern in chocks on deck, in preference to its merely hanging over the water from the davits.

Side davits on the small boat are not practical in general, as the first sea aboard will sweep the dinghy away. The dinghy, if it can be accommodated on deck, is best stowed about amidships and on the center line, overturned, if possible. Methods of decking the small boat are shown in Figure 113.

The most practical davits for the small cruiser are the ones of the round bar or radial type. A modification of the quadrant type, in which the davits hinge inboard and deliver the davited boat directly over its skids, is in use but cannot always be handled by one man.

114. With the small boat actually on board, it should always be provided with its own permanently secured skids and hold-down arrangement.

If the boat is carried upright, the skids take the outside shape of the sections at which they grip the boat and are padded to minimize chafing. These skids fold to the deck to facilitate handling the boat. They should always be high enough to permit mopping the deck under the secured boat; say, at least 10 inches.

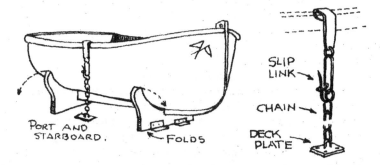

Figure 114. Chocking a Small Boat on Deck

A boat carried this way is held down by gripes which are easily cast off by releasing the locking link (*see* Figure 114). A boat cover must be provided, rigged over a ridgepole. It is usually fitted with canvas straps passing under the boat for lashing down.

A boat carried upside down needs chocks as well as some method of lashing to the deck. Unless the boat is of canvas-covered or plywood construction, a cover is desirable to prevent undue drying of the planking. On the sailboat a cover is necessary to prevent soiling sails and running rigging.

Modern yacht designers have recognized the dinghy and its problems as a serious handicap to successful cruising and are gradually coming to include the dinghy and making provisions for its stowage in the original design. This is accomplished by adjusting sail or deck plans to accommodate a small boat. Pram-type dinghies which fit over a part of the trunk, or become part of the cockpit or the deck, have been tried with some success.

Launching from a Ship

115. The launching of a heavy life boat presents special problems. Launching mechanism may be quadrantal davits, gravity davits or the common radial davits. The first two types operate by means of gears or levers which place the boat in position for lowering. The radial davits require careful maneuvering and drill in order to have them function to their designed purpose. Figure 115 gives the steps in diagrammatic form.

When the boat is swung out ready for lowering it should be in such condition as to become waterborne without further effort. The cover should be removed and it, with the spreaders, stowed within the boat, the boat plug in, the painter lead forward and outboard of all encumbrances, rudder hung and Jacob's ladder ready to drop into the boat when afloat.

If the boat is to be carried swung out for some time before launching, the strongback should be relashed to the davits and the boat lashed to the strongback by gripes. It is usual to leave the boat plug out if the boat is to be carried swung out. If an immediate launching is contemplated lash the strongback out of the way to some part of the ship if there is time; if not, cast it overboard as far clear of the side as possible.

Handling Boats Under Oars

Frapping lines leading from the lower (or movable) block of each fall will prevent the boat from swinging in a seaway or in the case of a severe outboard list. Such lines should lead from the swivel of the block or from a bight taken around the fall and should be handled from the boat deck.

Lowering is accomplished by paying out the boat falls from a sitting position and with the heels braced if possible. Gloves should be worn to avoid rope burns and the falls should be properly turned on a cleat to avoid a quick drop. The Jacob's ladder should be payed out as the boat is lowered from between the davits to the midships of the boat. If the ship has headway the after end of the boat should be a trifle lower than the forward end and should reach the water first.

Figure 115A. Launching a Davited Boat

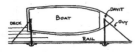

1. Clear Away. Falls are manned and the boat raised several inches above the chocks. Falls belayed. Chocks folded or knocked out. The after guy is cast off. (Boat plug checked.)

2. Launch Aft. The boat is swung forward, helped by a haul on the forward guy, and as it clears the after davit the forward guy is let go. Without loss of motion, the next step—

3. Bear out Aft. Haul away after guy—is completed. The stern is swung out.

4. Launch Forward. The boat is pushed aft, helped by a haul on the after guy.

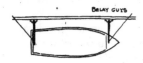

5. Bear out Forward. The boat is pushed outboard and both fore-and-aft guys securely belayed. The boat then can be lowered away.

(If the boat has been lashed to a strong back, the spar must first be removed from the davits before attempting to launch overboard.)

Releasing gear should be operated *before* the boat is completely waterborne and when the ship has reached the limit of a downward roll. If the ship has way on, the proper rigging of the sea painter from the boat to the ship will see the boat lying parallel to the ship, riding easy. Crashing may be avoided by use of the boat's rudder, putting the helm toward the ship slightly but not enough to cause a wild outward sheer and consequent danger of swamping or capsizing. The crew may board by the ladder or by sliding down the falls.

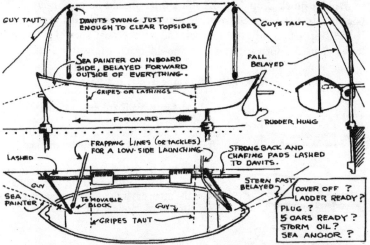

Figure 115B. Life Boat Swung out Ready for Emergency Lowering

Way is made by placing two oars ready for use and hauling ahead on the painter. When the painter is "up and down" it is cut smartly, the rudder put smartly away from the ship and the oars put into use. Get away from the ship at once on a right angle course to avoid propeller suction and to make room for other boats.

Whenever possible launch from the lee side or from the lowest side.

Always release the stern falls first when the ship has headway on.

If launching from the low side of a listed ship no special instructions are required save to rig frapping lines to the falls.

If launching from the high side of a listed ship keep a strain on the falls while the boat gripes are cast off lest the boat slide to the low side. A "skate" of some design is necessary to launch from the high side so that the boat will clear extending members of the ship, port hole rims, bolts and plate edges and will not capsize as it is lowered. If the boat is not equipped with the usual iron midship skate the strongback or another spar may be lashed along the inboard gunwale as a jury skate. It is almost hopeless to attempt to launch from the high side without a skate.

Rules Published by the Royal National Lifeboat Institution on the Management of Open Rowing Boats in a Surf: Beaching Them, Etc.

116. As a general rule, speed must be given to a boat rowing against a heavy surf.

Indeed, under some circumstances, her safety will depend on the utmost possible speed being attained on meeting a sea.

For, if the sea be really heavy, and the wind blowing a hard onshore gale, it can only be by the utmost exertions of the crew that any headway can be made. The great danger, then, is that an approaching heavy sea may carry the boat away on its front, and turn it broadside on, or up-end it, either effect being immediately fatal. A boat's only chance in such a case is to obtain such way as shall enable her to pass end-on, through the crest of the sea, and leave it as soon as possible behind her. Of course if there be a rather heavy surf, but no wind, or the wind offshore, and opposed to the surf, as is often the case, a boat might be propelled so rapidly through it that her bow would fall more suddenly and heavily after topping the sea than if her way had been checked; and it may therefore only be when the sea is of such magnitude, and the boat of such a character, that there may be a chance of the former carrying her back before it, that full speed should be given to her.

It may also happen that, by careful management under such circumstances, a boat may be made to avoid the sea, so that each wave may break ahead of her, which may be the only chance of safety in a small boat; but if the shore be flat, and the broken water extend to a great distance from it, this will often be impossible.

The following general rules for rowing to seaward may therefore be relied on:

1. If sufficient command can be kept over a boat by the skill of those

on board her, avoid or "dodge" the sea if possible, so as not to meet it at the moment of its breaking or curling over.

2. Against a head gale and heavy surf, get all possible speed on a boat on the approach of every sea which cannot be avoided.

If more speed can be given to a boat than is sufficient to prevent her being carried back by a surf, her way may be checked on its approach, which will give her an easier passage over it.

On Running before a Broken Sea, or Surf, to the Shore

117. The one great danger, when running before a broken sea, is that of broaching-to. To that peculiar effect of the sea, so frequently destructive of human life, the utmost attention must be directed.

The cause of a boat's broaching-to, when running before a broken sea or surf, is that her own motion being in the same direction as that of the sea, whether it be given by the force of oars or sails, or by the force of the sea itself, she opposes no resistance to it, but is carried before it. Thus, if a boat be running with her bow to the shore, and her stern to the sea, the effect of a surf or roller, on its overtaking her, is to throw up the stern, and as a consequence to depress the bow; if she then has sufficient inertia (which will be proportional to weight) to allow the sea to pass her, she will in succession pass through the descending, the horizontal, and the ascending positions, as the crest of the wave passes successively her stern, her midships, and her bow in the reverse order in which the same positions occur to a boat propelled to seaward against a surf. This may be defined as the safe mode of running before a broken sea.

But if a boat, on being overtaken by a heavy surf, has not sufficient inertia to allow it to pass her, the first of the three positions above enumerated alone occurs—her stern is raised high in the air and the wave carries the boat before it on its front or unsafe side, sometimes with frightful velocity, the bow all the time being deeply immersed in the hollow of the sea, where the water, being stationary or comparatively so, offers a resistance, while the crest of the sea, having the actual motion which causes it to break, forces onward the stern or rear end of the boat.

A boat will, in this position, sometimes aided by careful oar-steerage, run a considerable distance until the wave has broken and expended itself. But it will often happen that if the bow be low, it will be driven

Handling Boats Under Oars

under water, when the buoyancy being lost forward, while the sea presses on the stern, the boat will be thrown (as it is termed) end-over-end; or if the bow be high, or it be protected as in most lifeboats by a bow air chamber, so that it does not become submerged, so that the resistance forward, acting on one bow, will slightly turn the boat's head, and the force of the surf being transferred to the opposite quarter, she will in a moment be turned round broadside by the sea and be thrown by it on her beam-ends, or altogether capsized. It is in this manner that most boats are upset in a surf, especially on flat coasts; and in this way many lives are lost annually among merchant seamen when attempting to land, after being compelled to desert their vessels.

Hence it follows that the management of a boat, when landing through a heavy surf, must, so far as possible, be assimilated to that when proceeding to seaward against one, at least so far as to stop her progress shoreward at the moment of being overtaken by a heavy sea, and thus enabling it to pass her. There are different ways of effecting this object:

1. By turning a boat's head to the sea before entering the broken water, and then backing in stern foremost, pulling a few strokes ahead to meet each heavy sea, and then again backing astern. If a sea be really heavy, and a boat small, this plan will be generally the safest, as a boat can be kept more under command when the full force of the oars can be used against a heavy surf than by backing them only.

2. If rowing to shore with the stern to seaward, by backing all the oars on the approach of a heavy sea, and rowing ahead again as soon as it has passed to the bow of the boat, thus rowing in on the back of the wave; or, as is practiced in some lifeboats, placing the after-oarsmen with their faces forward, and making them row back at each sea on its approach.

3. If rowed in bow foremost, by towing astern a pig of ballast or a large stone, or a large basket, or canvas bag termed a *drogue* or *drag,* made for the purpose, the object of each being to hold the boat's stern back, and to prevent her being turned broadside to the sea or broaching-to.

Drogues are in common use by the boatmen on the Norfolk coast; they are conical-shaped bags of about the same form and proportionate length and breadth as a candle extinguisher, about two feet wide at the mouth and four and a half feet long. They are towed with the mouth foremost by a stout rope, a small line, termed a tripping line, being fast to the apex or pointed end. When towed with the mouth foremost, they fill with water and offer a considerable resistance, thereby holding back the stern; by letting go the stouter rope and retaining the smaller line, their position is reversed, when they collapse, and can be readily hauled into the boat.

Drogues are chiefly used in sailing boats, when they serve both to check a boat's way and to keep her end on to the sea. They are, however, a great source of safety in rowing boats, and the rowing lifeboats of the National Lifeboat Institution are now all provided with them.

A boat's sail bent to a yard and towed astern loosed, the yard being attached to a line capable of being veered, hauled, or let go, will act in some measure as a drogue, and will tend greatly to break the force of the sea immediately astern the boat.

Heavy weights should be kept out of the extreme ends of a boat; but when rowing before a heavy sea the best trim is deepest by the stern, which prevents the stern from being readily thrown on one side by the sea.

A boat should be steered by an oar over the stern, or on one quarter when running before a sea, as the rudder will then at times be of no use. If the rudder be shipped, it should be kept amidships on a sea breaking over the stern.

The following general rules may therefore be depended on when running before, or attempting to land through, a heavy surf or broken water:

1. As far as possible avoid each sea by placing the boat where the sea will break ahead or astern her.

2. If the sea be very heavy, or if the boat be very small, and especially if she have a square stern, bring her bow round to seaward and back her in, rowing ahead against each heavy surf that cannot be avoided sufficiently to allow it to pass the boat.

3. If it be considered safe to proceed to the shore bow foremost, back the oars against each sea on its approach, so as to stop the boat's way through the water as far as possible, and if there is a drogue, or any other instrument in the boat that may be used as one, tow it astern to aid in keeping the boat end on to the sea, which is the chief object in view.

4. Bring the principal weights in the boat toward the end that is to seaward, but not to the extreme end.

5. If a boat, worked by both sails and oars, be running under sail for the land through a heavy sea, her crew should, under all circumstances, unless the beach be quite steep, take down her masts and sails before entering the broken water, and take her to land under oars alone, as above described.

If she sails only, her sails should be much reduced, a half-lowered foresail or other small headsail being sufficient.

Beaching or Landing through a Surf

118. The running before a surf or broken sea and the beaching or landing of a boat are two distinct operations; the management of boats, as above recommended, has exclusive reference to running before a surf where the shore is so flat that the broken water extends to some distance from the beach. Thus, on a very steep beach, the first heavy fall of broken water will be on the beach itself, while on some very flat shores there will be a broken water as far as the eye can reach, sometimes extending to even four or five miles from the land. The outermost line of broken water, on a flat shore, where the waves break in three or four fathoms of water, is the heaviest, and therefore the most dangerous, and when it has been passed through in safety, the danger lessens as the water shoals, until, on nearing the land, its force is spent and its power harmless. As the character of the sea is quite different on steep and flat shores, so is the customary management of boats on landing different in the two situations. On the flat shore, whether a boat be run or backed in, she is kept straight before or end to the sea until she is fairly aground, when each surf takes her farther in as it overtakes her, aided by the crew, who will then generally jump out to lighten her, and drag her in by her sides. As above stated, the sail will, in this case, have been previously taken in if set, and the boat will have been rowed or backed in by oars alone.

On the other hand, on the steep beach, it is the general practice, in a boat of any size, to retain speed right on to the beach, and in the act of landing, whether under oars or sail, to turn the boat's bow half round toward the direction from which the surf is running, so that she may be thrown on her broadside up the beach, when abundance of help is usually at hand to haul her as quickly as possible out of the reach of the sea. In such situations, we believe, it is nowhere the practice to back a boat in stern foremost under oars, but to row in under full speed as above described.

NOTE: Most American authorities disapprove of the method of turning the bow half around toward the direction from which the surf is running, as described in the foregoing paragraph. The United States Coast Guard does not use such a method, nor do fishermen along the American coast. Most American coast boatmen prefer to beach by coming in fast and catching a chance to ride in on the back of a sea, letting the momentum carry them well up on the beach.

119. Beaching the small boat, up to 100 pounds or so, presents no difficulties, except in surf or heavy seas. Within limitations the remarks in paragraph 118 relating to the beaching of large pulling boats relate to small boats also. However, it is foolhardy to attempt beaching the small, light dinghy of ten or twelve feet in length in heavy surf conditions unless it is of undisputed seaworthy design and build. The various dory types might possibly fall into this class; any boat with a broad transom stern decidedly does not.

Sometimes a landing can be successfully made stern first, keeping the bows to the incoming seas and the weights slightly toward the bow. Headway and steerageway must be maintained under any conditions. Such a landing would probably only be made under emergency conditions, and the rower or passengers should be equipped with life preservers and resigned to a ducking and possible loss of the boat and/or its equipment.

120. The actual handling of the small boat on the beach is not particularly difficult, especially with man power available. Alone, the boat's safe removal to a point beyond danger may present some problems. Some hints for handling follow:

1. Use rollers (logs, branches, tubular fenders, large tin cans, etc.) if at all possible. Oars, with the blade end boosted slightly by riding on a driftwood stringer or another oar, can sometimes be made to work.

2. A boat will slide easily on wet kelp, or other seaweed, or on dry marsh grass.

3. Push the boat, never pull.

4. A fairly heavy boat can be "jogged"; i. e., lift one end and carry

ahead, pivoting on the remaining end; then lift the pivot end and repeat.

5. Always secure the boat to a stake or a rock, no matter how high on the beach. If on a rocky shore, with danger of the tide rising, boost the boat up on its oars, using them as beams spanning a low spot between high-flanking rocks.

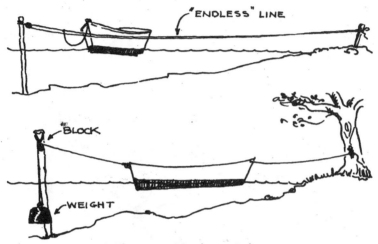

Figure 120. Mooring to Stakes

6. Hide the oars or lock them in the boat. Leave a note or some other indication showing the Coast Guard patrol or police that the boat is not abandoned nor shipwrecked.

121. The boat which is regularly beached or taken ashore upon landing should be handled by gear designed especially for that purpose. A dock or a float should be provided with a wide flush roller to facilitate the hauling to a safe position. Where there is a great rise and fall in the tide a "dinghy launch" serves well. The boat is usually handled by a tackle and possibly a small winch or capstan. (Figure 121A.)

122. Carrying boats on public highways. It is generally dangerous to carry even very small boats on the roof of a passenger car, especially at high speeds. In some states it is forbidden—and wisely.

The common carrying devices make use of gear which (a) grips a certain part of the car, usually the drip gutters, or (b) attaches by means of rubber suction caps. Both are weak in that they do not provide for the great strains of windage. The pocketing effect of an overturned boat being driven into the wind or against wind of the car's own making is tremendous and frequently has resulted in serious accidents.

The safest method of transporting boats over highways is by the use of a boat trailer. Such a trailer must be heavy enough to amply

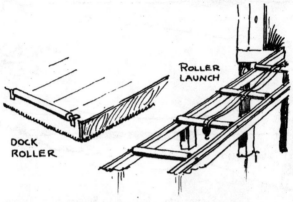

Figure 121A

carry the boat and its gear (spars, oars, ground tackle, or outboard motor) and be provided with a self-gripping cradle and adequate lash-down devices.

In all states the following regulations apply to trailers:

1. They must be rubber-tired.
2. They must be attached to the towing car by a "hitch" of approved design and manufacture. (Some states require chain attachment in addition, in case of failure of the hitch.)
3. They must be licensed and their license plates displayed.
4. They must carry an electrically lighted taillight, stoplight, and license-plate light. (Some states further require a tail-reflector light.)
5. They must not exceed eight feet maximum width. (Boats wider than this require special permits for each haul, secured generally from police bureaus or state highway departments.)

Handling Boats Under Oars

(In some states, trailers over certain weights, or having four wheels, require their own braking systems operated by the car driver.)

123. Boats shipped by rail, if heavy, must be provided with a suit-able cradle mounted on skids. Handling, placing on the car, and chocking are usually done by the railroad company and always under

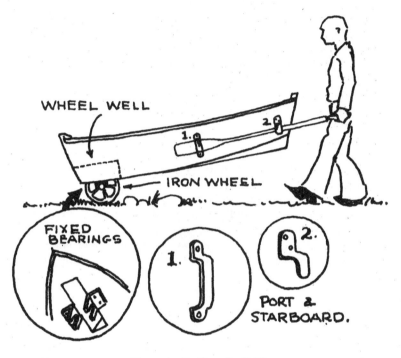

Figure 121B. Trundle Skiff

the direction of an experienced foreman. Before rolling, they must be examined and approved by a representative of the freight department.

Tanks must be empty and no gasoline is permitted to be carried aboard. Unless especially insured, the contents of a boat (gear, navi-gating equipment, stores, etc.) are not covered by ordinary trans-portation insurance. Ordinarily, the contents of boats carried on a flat car must be removed from the boat. Watchmen or boat tenders, in the employ of the shipper, may not sleep or live on the boat while it is being transported. Sometimes, such a tender may travel in the caboose, paying regular passenger fare.

Small boats shipped by rail need not be crated but must be covered, usually by a burlap wrapper, sewn on. Husky, sharpie-type boats and dories are sometimes shipped without any wrapping.

Spars, shipped separately, must be wrapped and protected. Rigging should be removed, especially blocks, spreaders, and winches.

In shipping via express, the rules of the express company apply and may vary from the requirements of railroad freight departments.

Under special conditions, such as in the case of a large shipment of dinghies to a port on the racing circuit, or outboard racers, or a flotilla of canoes shipping against the current or around rapids, exceptions are made and usual rules do not apply.

In preparing a boat for railroad shipment, seal every space against cinders and usual railway dust. Large glass areas should be reinforced or braced. Reduce the boat to its barest form, removing cowl ventilators, bowsprits, military masts, etc. Awnings and dodger cloths should be removed. If the hull travels wet, that is, soaked and the planks fully swollen, vibration and jarring will do less damage to caulking and fastenings than when dry. A light cover over the boat, securely fastened, will not only keep the boat reasonably free of cinders but will help to prevent the too rapid drying out of the planking.

GLOSSARY

The recognized nomenclature of the principal parts of boats and their fittings is as follows:

Apron.—A timber fitted abaft the stem to reinforce the stem and to give a sufficient surface on which to land the hood ends of the planks.

Beams.—Transverse supports running from side to side to support the deck.

Bilge.—The part of the bottom, on each side of the keel, on which the boat would rest if aground.

Binding strake.—A strake of planking, usually thicker than other planks, fitted next to and under the sheer strake.

Blade, oar.—The broad flattened part of an oar as distinguished from the loom.

Handling Boats Under Oars

Boat falls.—Blocks and tackle with which the boats are hoisted aboard at davits.

Boat hook.—A pole with a blunt hook on the end to aid in landing operations or hauling alongside.

Boat plug.—A screwed metal plug fitted in the bottom planking of the boat at the lowest point to drain the bilges when boat is out of the water.

Bottom boards.—The fore-and-aft planks secured to the frames, or to floor beams, forming the floor of the boat, frequently removable.

Braces, rudder, upper, and lower.—Strips of metal secured to the rudder, the forward ends of which fit over the rudder hanger on the stern-post, thus securing the rudder and forming a pivot upon which the rudder swings.

Breaker.—A small cask for carrying potable water.

Breasthook.—A wood or metal knee fitted behind the stem structure.

Capping.—The fore-and-aft finishing piece on top of the clamp and sheer strake, at the frame heads, in an open boat.

Carling.—A fore-and-aft beam at hatches.

Chock.—A metal casting used as a fair-lead for a mooring line or anchor chain.

Clamp.—A main longitudinal strengthening member under the deck in decked-over boats and at the gunwale in open boats.

Cleat.—A horned casting for belaying lines.

Cockpit.—A compartment, usually for passengers, in an open boat.

Deadwood.—Timber built on top of the keel or shaft log at either end of the boat to afford a firm fastening for the frames and to connect the keel to the end timbers.

Fenders.—Portable wooden or rope sennit bumpers hung over the side during landings to protect the hull.

Flat.—A walking surface in the engine room or any special platform, such as the coxswain's flat.

Floors.—The transverse timbers which reinforce the frames and carry the strength athwartships across the keel.

Footlings.—Bottom boards or walking flats attached to the insides of the frames on boats where deep floors are not fitted.

Foresheets.—The portion of the boat forward of the foremost thwart.

Frames.—The ribs of the boat; curved timbers, frequently steam-bent, secured to the keel and extending upward to the gunwale or deck.

Garboard.—The lowest strake of outside planking next to the keel.

Grapnel.—A small multiple-fluked anchor used in dragging or grappling operations.

Gripes.—The fitting used to secure a boat in its stowage position on board ship. For boats secured at the davit heads, gripes are made of tarred hemp woven with a wood mat, backed with canvas, to hold the boat against the strongback. For lifeboats, the lower ends of the gripes are usually fitted with a slip hook. For boats secured in cradles, the gripes are usually of metal, tightened with turnbuckles, and arranged to prevent the boats from lifting from the cradles when the deck becomes awash.

Gudgeons.—Small metal fittings, similar to eyebolts, secured to the sternpost of very small boats on which the rudder hangs. Used in place of the rudder hanger of larger boats.

Gunwale.—The upper edge of the side of an open boat.

Hanger, rudder.—A vertical strip of metal, secured to the sternpost, forming the traveler upon which the rudder braces are secured.

Hoisting pads.—Metal fittings inside the boat often attached to the keel to take the hoisting slings or hoisting rods.

Horn timber.—The after deadwood (often called counter timber) fastening the shaft log and transom knee together.

Keel.—The principal timber of a boat, extending from stem to stern at the bottom of the hull and supporting the whole frame.

Keel stop.—A small metal fitting on the keel, at the after end, to act as a stop in locating the boat in a fore-and-aft position on the keel rest when stowing the boat in the cradle.

Keelsons.—Fore-and-aft structural timbers either above or outboard of the keel.

Knee.—A shaped timber for connecting construction members installed at an angle to each other. Some knees are sawn from straight-grained wood, while in other cases the grain follows the natural bend of the tree at a limb or root.

Leather.—The portion of an oar which rests in the rowlock. This is sometimes covered with canvas, but is usually covered with leather.

Loom.—Rounded portion of an oar between the blade and handle.

Norman pin.—A metal pin fitted in a towing post or bitt for belaying the line.

Painter.—A rope used in the bow for towing or for securing the boat.

Pintles.—Small straight pieces of metal secured to the rudder and fitting in the gudgeons on the sternpost of very small boats, thus supporting the rudder. Pintles and gudgeons are used in place of the rudder braces of larger boats.

Plank-sheer.—The outermost deck plank at the side.

Risings.—The fore-and-aft stringers inside a boat, secured to the frames, on which the thwarts rest.

Rowlocks.—Forked pieces of metal in which the leathers of oars rest

Handling Boats Under Oars

while pulling. *Sunken rowlocks* are those which are set down in the gunwale of the boat. *Swivel rowlocks* rotate, the shank of the rowlock fitting in a socket in the gunwale.

Sheer.—The line of form at the side which the gunwale or deck edge follows in profile.

Sheer strake.—The uppermost strake of planking at the side following the line of sheer.

Side fender.—A longitudinal timber projecting beyond the outside line of the hull planking, often metal faced, to protect the hull.

Slings.—Gear made of wire rope and close-linked chain for handling boats at booms or cranes.

Spars.—Masts, booms, and gaffs upon which, when stepped in the boat, the sails are spread.

Steering rowlock.—A form of swivel rowlock, fitted near the stern of a whaleboat or motor whaleboat, in which the steering oar is shipped; sometimes called a crutch.

Stem.—The upright timber in the forward part of a boat, joined to the keel by a knee.

Stem band.—A metal facing or cutwater fitted on the stempost.

Stem heel (The forward deadwood).—A timber, often called the sole piece, used to connect the stem knee to the keel.

Stern fast.—A stern painter for use in securing the stern of a boat.

Stern hook.—Same as breasthook, for stern on a double-ended boat.

Sternpost.—The principal vertical piece of timber at the after end of a boat, its lower end fastened to the keel or shaft log by a stern knee.

Stern sheets.—The space in the boat abaft the thwarts.

Strakes.—Continuous lines of fore-and-aft planking. Each line of planking is known as a strake.

Stretchers.—Athwartship, movable pieces against which the oarsmen brace their feet in pulling.

Stringers, bilge.—Longitudinal strengthening timbers inside the hull.

Strongback.—The spar between the davits to which a boat is griped.

Tarpaulin.—A waterproof fabric cover to keep stores dry while being transported.

Tholepin.—A pin fitted in the gunwale plank for use in place of a rowlock. Used with Manila ring about five inches in diameter, called a *tholepin grommet.*

Thrum mats.—Mats made of a small piece of canvas, with short strands of rope yarn sewed on them, called *thrumming*. These are placed between the rowlocks and the oars to prevent noise in pulling.

Tiller.—A bar or lever, fitted fore and aft in the rudder head, by which the rudder is moved.

Towing bitts (Often called towing posts).—A vertical timber securely fastened for use in towing or mooring.

Trailing lines.—Small lines secured to the boat and around the oars to prevent the latter from getting adrift when trailed from swivel rowlocks.

Transom.—The planking across the stern in a transomed boat.

Yoke.—Athwartship piece fitting over the rudder head, by which the rudder is moved by yoke ropes when the tiller is not shipped.

CPSIA information can be obtained
at www.ICGtesting.com
Printed in the USA
LVHW041555040520
654951LV00005B/1275